The Voice of God Within
By Elizabeth A. Van Cleve

Contents

Acknowledgments

I am grateful to:

The voice of God within, who has loved, guided, taught, encouraged and inspired me- who has been a source of comfort in the darkest nights and has never, ever left me.

My gentle husband, for his love and care, and his patience with my long hours of writing

My girlfriends, including my daughters, who are my support system and have been brave ambassadors of the voice within their own hearts

My son Shane, because he is just simply an amazing young man

All of you who read my blog and encourage me in my writing endeavors- you know who you are

Ashley Well's online class, "31 Days to Write Your EBook" which was instrumental helped me to complete the first edition of this book

My sweet friend Vanessa, who reached out her entire heart and soul to be a comfort, support and friend to me when I first left church; who was the first to read this book and tell me how good she thought it was

My dear friend Zoya- who, by her example has taught me courage, fortitude and how beautiful a soul can be when they listen to the voice of God in their own heart

My therapist Elaine- for helping me to realize that it is really okay to be who I am and right where I am right now

For my readers

- In order to receive the maximum benefit and enlightenment that this book offers, the personal exercises are imperative.

- Although I recognize God as a Spirit and not a *he* or a *she* but rather the very essence of all life, yet for lack of another vocabulary word, I often defer to *him* throughout this book.

- This book tells about my own personal spiritual journey and how I experienced it. I talk about the religion/church I was involved with for many years and the reasons behind why I eventually left religion. This is neither to defame nor to shame any particular religious body, including the one I left. I understand by experience that religion is a stepping stone and has many benefits. However to bring out the issues clearly that I am dealing with here, I focus more intently on the *unhealthy* aspects of religion and the church I attended and served in. The people I fellowshipped with generally have good hearts and are doing the best that they can with what they understand and the tools that they have.

- Many of the thoughts throughout this book will overlap and there is good reason behind this. It is because many of the ideas presented may be very revolutionary to the reader and will need to be brought from several different angles in order to break through the religious filters that we are all subject to one degree or another.

Dedication

To the universal oneness of Spirit and all that it encompasses!

Introduction

What if you could be encapsulated- dropped into a capsule of love and light, where all that you could see is the beauty and light of your own spirit; then, when you emerge from this encapsulation, you are just glowing and radiant? God wants to immerse you in the Spirit. He wants to encapsulate you in love and light. He wants to show you the beauty of your own soul.

The Bible tells us that Moses went up alone onto a mountain and met with God. High up on that mountain, God answered Moses' inquiry of who he should tell people that God was? He answered, *"I am that I am."* Thousands of years later, Christ told the people, *"I am the bread of life. . . I am the truth, the way, the life . . . I am the living water."* Have you given much thought to the two little, but so very powerful words, "I AM"?

So many People have been looking for God in the wrong places. They keep going to church, believing that it is there they will feel closer to God; there, they will learn all about God, and be with good people that know God. Yet "church" endlessly fragments into more and more cliques and controls and confuses.

God said to Moses, *"I Am that I AM."*

When Christ met the Samaritan woman at the well, she said to him, *"Our fathers worshipped in this mountain; and you say, in Jerusalem is the place where men ought to worship."* (John 4:20) The woman was opening up a spiritual argument with Christ about where the right place to worship truly was. The Samaritans were divided against the Jews; they had religious division- just as we continue to see within religion today. But Christ had an answer for her that she was not expecting, and he has the same answer today when we are asking the question, **where is the right place to find God?** Christ said to her, *"Woman, believe me, the hour is coming,*

7

when you will neither in this mountain, nor at Jerusalem worship the Father. You do not even know what you are worshipping. We know what we worship, for salvation is of the Jews; but the hour comes, and is now, when the true worshippers shall worship the Father in spirit and in truth. For the Father seeks such to worship him. God is a spirit; and they that worship Him, must worship him in spirit and in truth." (John 4:21-24)

Jesus put to silence the very basis of her argument; he broke down her wall of division. He basically said, neither one is right- this wall of religious division has to go. This is not what God cares about. What God wants is a true worshipper- someone who is willing to be encapsulated in His light and love- someone who recognizes that God is spirit and *it is within our spirit that we meet the great I AM!*

God wants us to understand what it is to be one with Spirit. Christ said, *"The kingdom of God is within."* Religion is *without* and it builds walls around a set of beliefs that separates itself from other religious bodies and claims to be the ambassador of I AM. Once you put a name over door, once you become a part of a religious sect, you are defining who you are and *who you are not.* You are dividing yourself from part of humanity.

Revelations 18 speaks of *"Mystery Babylon"* as the *"habitation of devils and a hold every foul spirit and a cage of every unclean and hateful bird."* It tells us that all nations have committed fornication with her. We may look at this as a depiction of religious systems; they become cages of men who believe that they must be a part of a religion in order to be accepted of God. The media has exposed the myriads of devils that inhabit so many of them and history bears witness to the enormous bloodshed all done in the name of religious belief systems. All nations have committed spiritual fornication with her. All nations are filled with religious systems, and so many of the people within, worship the *system* above God; as Christ said to the woman at the well, they cease to even know the true I AM. They become entangled in their doctrines, creeds, rules, programs, regulations and forms, and many believe that these things make them superior to all other people. They have made quite a market out of the whole religious system, just as Revelations describes.

In a book titled, "The Soul of the Indian; an Interpretation, by Charles A. Eastman," it speaks of the early Native American Indian's perspective on the Christian white man. Eastman writes;

"There was undoubtedly much in the primitive Christianity to appeal to this man, and Jesus' hard sayings to the rich would have been entirely comprehensible to him. Yet the religion that is preached in our churches and practiced by our congregations, with its element of display and self-aggrandizement, its active proselytism, and its open contempt of all religions but its own, was for a long time extremely repellent. To his simple mind, the professionalism of the pulpit, the paid exhorter, the moneyed church, was an unspiritual and unedifying thing, and it was not until his spirit was broken and his moral and physical constitution undermined by trade and conquest and strong drink, that Christian missionaries ever obtained any real hold upon him." (Page 20)

Christ taught us that God wants us to worship him within our spirit and in truth. Yet here, history speaks of religion needing to *break* the spirit and moral of the Indian in order to proselyte him. How sad! This has become the case with so many people, not just the Indian. Religion and its influence have broken their true spirit- their inner connection with God, and has sold them the strong drink of delusion. We understand that not all churches are wicked and wrong. Some can be beneficial. However, as Christ was demonstrating to the woman at the well, a church location or denomination is not where God is to be found, nor where his voice is heard.

Without learning to discern God's voice within our own spirit, we become easy prey for spiritual wolves and entangled in all kinds of superstitious beliefs that have nothing to do with God. We will continue to look for "signs" without, of what God is doing in our lives or how he is leading. We can make irrational judgments about others and their misfortunes, believing that it is God's way of "dealing with them." When things are going good for us, we will believe God is pleased with us and we are connected. But when life takes that turn for the worse, we can easily get lost in doubts and fears about what God is now doing.

God is calling you back to I AM- to oneness with Spirit! Will you take the time to *listen* and to *hear* the great I AM speaking within your own heart? If so, grab a pen and journal and get ready to take an amazing journey into the core of your own soul- the seat of the great I AM!

Chapter 1

Beautiful YOU!

"You are beautiful I know, because I made you."

-God

"Are not five sparrows sold for two pennies? Yet not one of them is forgotten by God. Indeed, the very hairs of your head are all numbered. Don't be afraid; you are worth more than many sparrows." Luke 12:6-7

There is tremendous value in your soul. You are so unique that out of over seven-billion people that live on this planet, you could be identified by your fingerprint alone. You are a special treasure to God, so intimately known, that every strand of your hair is numbered. You have incredible value and individuality. Truly it is a travesty how many people want to be, hope to be, strive to be, like somebody else. If only we could see in ourselves what a loving mother sees in her newborn child- the beauty, the perfection, the potential. *If only we could see ourselves as God sees us.*

I have sat under many preachers who have brought mixed messages concerning my personal value. I have heard it preached on one hand that I was valuable to God and on another hand that I was nothing more than a worm and that God could easily replace me. I have heard that God loves and cherishes me so much that if I were the only one in this world, he would have still sent his son to die for me. But then I have heard that God hates sin and is preparing a horrible place of everlasting torture for those who don't "get right," or for those who dare to disobey him. It is a contradiction. I can never imagine preparing a place of endless torture for any of my children who refuse to "obey" me. How can one become intimately close to a God that may one day see fit to torcher them eternally?

What about our homes here on earth? What about this present time- this only place that we truly experience? How many of us have been born into homes where love is a foreigner, and where anger, hostility, and depression are constant companions? How many are born into families that place value, not on the soul, but on performance?

"Who do you think you are anyways?" The insolent query is hissed out of an irreverent parent's mouth onto a vulnerable child.

"You are nothing- worthless! If you died tomorrow, the world would go on just the same without you, as if you never even existed. You make my life miserable. I wish you had never been born."

Words like these are spewed out onto the defenseless child in his formative years, and for the rest of his life he carries the infected wound. And even without the words, actions can speak volumes of worthlessness into the soul of the child. Many feel unseen, unloved, abandoned, and hopeless. The child grows, ceaselessly searching for some sort of positive affirmation, some sense of validation and security. But the poisonous venom continues to weaken and damage his self-view until he even despairs of life itself.

"What's the point?" He wonders, *"What am I doing here?"*

Indeed, many dejected souls claim their own life every day. In fact, in the year 2010 over 38,000 people took their lives in the US alone. That averages at 105 suicides every day. Suicide is the second leading cause of death for ages 10-24. And this does not even include failed attempts. So many precious souls that came to the conclusion that they were so worthless, that they needed to permanently dispose of themselves- *destroy their own life.* That is pretty intense.

Christ came with a very important message from God. He said in so many words, *God loves YOU! God wants YOU! God desires a personal friendship with YOU! God wants to be one with YOU!* In our most intimate earthly relationships two bodies merge together as one. A deep gratifying surge of ecstasy can be experienced between lovers. God wants to be even closer. Spirit desires to be one with you- God and you- the same- *no difference.*

The word "Christ" means *anointed one.* It is a title just as Doctor and Professor are titles. Like-so, originally it preceded the name- *Christ* Jesus. Only later after Jesus had long passed off the scene did it evolve into a name, Jesus Christ. The anointed are those who are perfectly aligned with God- they are masters. "Jesus" is the name given to a man born of the flesh. "Christ" is the title of what Jesus is- Jesus is Christ or, Jesus in anointed. Jesus Christ came to bring us into this same perfect alignment with God- where we have always belonged. Why? Because he VALUES us! To be anointed is to be one with God. Christ Elizabeth. God is Elizabeth. Elizabeth is God. *"Is it not written in your scriptures, ye are gods?"* ~Jesus (John 10:34)

You are here for a reason. You are here to learn something. And what you are here to learn, you are also here to teach. You have value beyond measure. No one else can ever have the unique perspective that you have. Your unique perspective is for you to share with other souls; and they are here to share their perspective. We are all students and we are all teachers- *all the time.* When you begin to come into alignment with Spirit (God) you will emerge like a butterfly from a cocoon into your most beautiful self. As you realize just what a treasure YOU are, and how intimately close God is, you will find constant companionship, friendship, love, and value. Let God immerse you into his spirit!

Exercise:

Dear reader,

I begin the first of this book with exercises designed to bolster your self-view and love for yourself because it is imperative, in order to really come to a place of trust in God's love, to really believe inside your own heart that you are completely 100% loveable just the way you are!

1. Go into the bathroom (or somewhere you can be alone in front of a mirror) shut the door and look at yourself in the mirror, straight in the eye and say to yourself, "I love you. I *LOVE* you. I love *YOU!*" Add your name to the end. "I love you...!" Say it as many times as you need to. Take note of your inner reaction to this exercise. Write about it in your journal. *Continue practicing this every morning.* As time goes by, you may even add your own personal sentimental variations such as, "You are so precious to me. You are the BEST friend I have ever had. I am so thankful for you!" and so on.
2. Begin a list in your journal of things you truly love or admire about yourself. Get creative! Maybe it's a birthmark, the way you laugh, or your clever sense of humor.
3. Plan to do something special for yourself each week. PLAN! Figure out the best day, time, place, etc.... call make reservations if necessary. Invite a friend you love to be with. But make sure this is a special day for YOU and something you love. Think about how you are feeling, what sounds like it would bring you the most joy? It may be getting a

pedicure, making yourself a special smoothie, or taking a break to read that book you've wanted to read. Tailor it to your personal lifestyle and desires.

4. Make a commitment to take care of yourself first. In the financial world, it has been said that to pay your-self first is a vital step in gaining a true foothold on money management. I believe that taking care of you *first* is vital to gaining a true foothold on a spiritually, physically and emotionally balanced life. Yes! You are worth it! Practice putting value on yourself by your actions.

5. Talk to God. Let Spirit know if you would like to be anointed-one with God. Before you close your eyes to sleep at night, repeat to yourself; *"I am one with Spirit. Spirit and I desire my highest good. Spirit and I are one."* Then wrap yourself in a warm blanket of love, let go of the day and fall to sleep.

Chapter 2

The Lie of Religion

"When you see one thing differently, you will see all things differently."

-A Course in Miracles

What did Jesus come into the world to do? Why did he die such a horrible and cruel death? And why did he rise from the dead? The answer, in its simplest and purest form is, LOVE! *"For God so LOVED the world..."* Because God loved the people of this world so much- he gave us Jesus, his only begotten Son. And whoever believes in him, whoever believes his message, whoever listens to him, whoever hears him, will not perish, but have eternal life. *"Oh death where is thy sting? The sting of death is sin."*

Sin basically means *separation from God*. God saw how disconnected the people of this world were from him- the source of light and love. And consequently, they were perishing. *"God is LOVE and in him is no darkness at all."* (1 John 1:5, 1 John 4:8) Separation from God is separation from love and light. The farther away from God you drift, the farther you are away from love and light.

In the Bible, God identified himself as, *"I AM!"*

Jesus said, *"I AM the bread of life"* (John 6:48)

Jesus came to turn our hearts back to God. He came to help us reconnect to the very source of all life. We, who were walking in darkness, who could not find our way, who had no understanding of why we are here, frantically trying to make sense of the senseless, grappling about for some sort of solace of love, of purpose- Christ came to reconnect us to the source of light. *"I AM the light."* He came to show us the way; *"I AM the way."* He came to bind our hearts to the one who is love; (1 John 4: 8, 16) He came to reconnect us to the great *"I AM"*!

Jesus came to save us- but, from what? He came to save us from sin. The word "sin" in its purest form means to *"miss"* or **to not be there**. To not be there is to miss out on life. It is death. Without connection to God, we are the walking dead. God, or Spirit, is the source of all life. Jesus came to save us from death. When we are dead we are *miss*ing out on life. Death means unconsciousness. *Mis*conduct happens when we try to go through life unconscious. We do things that we would otherwise not do if we were truly aware and alive. Common terms for consciousness are *being present* and *mindfulness*. To be separated from I AM is to be unaware of your true self. Socrates said, *"To know thyself is the beginning of wisdom."* **Sin is to miss**- it is to be separated from your true nature, your divine self.

So much of religion is *miss*ing the mark. Religious history has left a trail of *death*. Bloodshed has been used in pursuit of life, but as we all know, bloodshed doesn't give life, it destroys it. Jesus, through his death, reached out to mankind- He became a sacrifice in order to satisfy the law of the Israelites, which required blood to atone for *mis*conduct. Through his death he tore down the veil of ignorance that blinded us and separated us from God. Jesus' ultimate goal was to refocus us back to I AM *within*. To those who felt too ashamed to approach God, those who felt too unworthy to be thought as **one** with the great I AM, those who devalue their selves and those who believe they are so unlovable; through his suffering and death, Christ wrapped us up in eternal arms of love and light. Through his agony he declared a timeless message to the world- *God wants you back!*

But his death was not the way to life. His death was to satisfy the law-*men's* law that they felt so bound to keep. This law had kept them from connection to God, because it taught of a wrathful being that kept score of right and wrong, and the system gave certain men the power to define what right and wrong was. Jesus taught humanity that the Kingdom of God is not somewhere to be found; rather, the kingdom of God is within us. God is the giver of life and we need not that any man teach us, for the Spirit within will teach us as we learn to listen and hear.

In order for the lesson to come full circle, *Jesus had to die- because the law-* embedded in the minds of men, had to be satisfied if they were going to be able to trust a relationship with God. Jesus' sacrifice was not for God's sake, but for men's sake. For as long as men were conscious of a law that they knew they could never fully keep, they were bound under a spirit of *fear* and could not trust approaching God. But when Christ fulfilled the law, when he became sin and nailed it once and for all to the cross, they no longer had to keep spilling the blood of animals. After three days in the darkness of death he arose – This was to take FEAR away- the sting of death, the very point of oblivion that bound people to superstitious traditions. By the resurrection we learned that physical death is only transitory. It is spiritual death that brings all the human ills and woes. When we lose touch with Spirit, with I AM; we lose touch with *self*. We are spiritually unconscious, dead to this enchanting, rich and eternal life. We become displaced, unhappy, and without peace. The sting of death is sin- missing the mark. This was removed- the law that keeps people from listening within for the source of life.

The Bible gives account of a people who believed they were the special people of God. They recorded stories in which they believed God was either moving in their behalf or fighting against them, according to whether or not they were keeping a set of laws they believed to be given by God. They wrote of a King that would one day come and deliver them from all oppression. This King would come from the genealogy of King David; many had differing prophetic visions about futuristic happenings that were not easily decoded. There is much contention about the true origins of these writings, there authenticity, and what they all mean. But the general consensus in Christianity is that Jesus Christ was the historical figure who fulfilled these prophecies. Some people believe he was "God in the flesh." But perhaps, *God is in all our flesh* and to be mindful of God in our flesh, to be mindful of our true divine nature, to be anointed with the Holy Spirit, is to have eternal life.

John 10 records a story in which the Jews were gathered around Jesus trying to trick him into saying something that would indict him. In verse 30, Jesus tells them, *"I am my Father are one."* The Jews then picked up rocks to stone him with and when Jesus asked why, they said he had spoken blasphemy, making himself "one with God." Jesus replies to them; *"Is it not written in **your law**, I said, **you are gods**? If he called them gods, unto whom the word of God came, and the scripture cannot be broken; Why do you say of him, whom the Father has sanctified, and sent into the world, 'You speak blasphemy;' because I said, I am the Son of God? If I am not doing the works of my Father, then do not believe me. But if I do, though you do not believe me, believe the works: that you may know, and believe, that **the Father is in me, and I in him.**"*

Psalms 82:6 and Isaiah 41:23 both refer to men as being gods. Jesus was trying to teach them a universal truth, but the lie of religion had so brainwashed them, they were unable to hear what he was saying. He said to them, *God and I are one - we are the same.* We are not two separate beings. Then he went on to say, *"**You too are gods**. It's even written in YOUR law."* You see, He was giving them the exact same status as he had given himself. The only difference his anointing. He had the anointing; he had the Christ awareness- the awareness that he and God were exactly the same- *they were one.* Note what Jesus did *not* say; He did not say, *it is written in God's word,* or *it is written in God's law.* Rather, he said, *"It is written in **your law.**"*

He then went on to say, *Look, I am doing the works of God- the works of LOVE and LIGHT. Can you not you see that? Can you not understand the difference between the works of darkness and the works of light, or, the works of love from the works of hate?*

You see, there is a BIG lie within the majority of religion. Lies can be very destructive and this lie of religion has been heinous. This lie has been used to accuse, torment, and at times even torture and murder innumerable souls. This lie of religion is simple and yet complex. It is obvious and yet obscure. This lie of religion says that somewhere out there, somewhere outside *yourself*- you will find God. Consequently countless divisions of religious systems have been erected claiming themselves to be the place, the people, the teachings, the laws, the culture that you need to be *right* with God. The lie of religion has set up pinnacles of worship that claim authority on who God is, and has declared itself to be the mediator between God and man. This lie says that the *truth* is in a doctrine or right interpretation of the Bible.

I will now put forth an analogy. What if a very wealthy couple decided to go and seek out an orphan to take in as their own child; they determine to find a needy child from off the streets. They are successful and they bring this homeless orphan to their own abode with the intent to raise her as their very own. Although they know the beauty and value of this precious coveted child, and rejoice to have found her, yet there is much work to be done in the transitioning process from life on the streets to a wealthy home.

No doubt, first and foremost she would need a bath and a change of clothes. But that would be just the beginning. That little child only knows the ways of street living. She has no manners, no refinement; survival has been her only way of life. She is in constant "fight or flight" mode. Notwithstanding all the new luxury and devotion poured out upon her, she is going to feel like a fish out of water in this new environment. Though she has been cleaned up on the *outside*, and placed in a new environment, something extremely crucial has not yet changed- something that is on the *inside*. She still sees herself as a poor, ignorant, worthless, street urchin. ***Nothing that has taken place on the outside, has changed her self-view on the inside.*** Only through much patience, love, and nurturing, consistently over time, will her self-view begin to be altered for the better. Only by her consistently seeing and knowing that these new caretakers deeply value who she is on the inside, will she begin to believe in her own worth. This is a parable to reflect the one who is saved from a life of sin and separation from God.

Religion is on the *outside*. A person comes to church. They hear a fundamental message of salvation and repentance. This message teaches them to become aware of where they now are. This is good- awareness is imperative. The person repents and cleans up their life. They then attribute all that has passed to the *religion* rather than to the *connection* they made within their self to God. They now refocus their attention without- on the religious teachings and the people who bring them. And so the preacher begins to pound out, *"thus saith the Lord,"* over the pulpit. The preacher takes it upon himself to lay out the *"judgment"* - the NEW law, in a fearful and sometimes condescending message aimed toward cleaning up the filthy street way learned in life before "conversion." The preacher hears the "amens" and feels zealous, and believes them these to be a sign from God that he is "hitting the nail on the head." Well, he is hitting something all right- *and he is doing a lot of damage.* Something very subtle is being overlooked- that soul's *self-view!* Instead of being taught to love and trust their self and to trust the inner voice of the divine within, they are being drawn away to the death-trap once again of *missing the mark.*

That new convert who has a wounded soul, who's self-view has been so damaged and distorted, shrinks back in the pew, as the joy and happiness of connection to a loving God, day by day evaporates, and trust in God is replaced with a **fear** of God. That worthless self-view is now writhing under all the judgment and warnings of a wrathful God who is going to someday return and destroy those who would dare to do anything amiss. She desperately clings to Jesus as if any moment he would abandon her, even though Christ promised *never* to leave her. The message is full of fearful and woeful warnings and whippings believed to 'help' the new converts "measure up!" Their experience of God now becomes deduced to that of Mt Sinai. *"For they could not endure that which was commanded, And if so much as a beast touch the mountain, it shall be stoned, or thrust through with a dart: And so terrible was the sight, that Moses said, I exceedingly fear and quake:"* Hebrew 12:20-21

Fundamental religion has changed the Old Testament law and order, for a New Testament law and order. Religion at large has fed the wounded child the same damaging message he received in his formative years; *"You are bad! You are innately bad! You need to be fixed! There is something wrong with you!"* There is no abundant life in this. And by their new laws they have sacrificed the value of a **single** soul, for the system. Yet Jesus himself demonstrated the value of a single soul over and over again. And he taught us that the good shepherd will go so far as to leave his flock of 99 sheep, to go and fetch the one that is lost. So much of religion has replaced mercy and grace with law and order. Jesus told some,

22

"Go, learn what this means, I will have mercy and not sacrifice." (Matthew 9:13) God is not interested in all our sacrifices. He is interested in love and mercy and restoration. He is interested in relationship. God is a spirit.

Fundamental religion has taken letters, that early Christians wrote to one another, to admonish one another, during their time in history, according to their culture, as they struggled to learn and understand this new relationship with God, and they have transposed them as if they were written by the finger of God, in tables of stone; using these letters, they have attempted time and again to establish a new law and order. They have turned letters written by men no different than you and I, and made all kinds of "thou shalts," and "thou shalt nots" out of them. Consequently, we have the "Christian" mess we see in the world today- and throughout history. Each religion is trying to infer how to properly carry out this law and order, so as not to provoke the wrath of God. The foundation of most religion is not truth but rather FEAR!

This is SO missing the mark! Jesus never, ever came to establish a new law and order. He fulfilled the Hebrew law through his death and resurrection, so that we could reconnect to God. Christ came to tear down walls, not build them. But he especially came to remove the barrier between us and God- the law! The law could never make us perfect in God. Why? Because instead of listening to the WORD of God *within our own souls*, and allowing the WORD to be our guide, we ignore the WORD and study the law that is without- and when we do this we become further and further from Spirit and truth, further away from love and light, and closer to death and darkness; *"For Christ is the end of the law of righteousness to everyone that believes."* (Romans 10:4)

Christ came to put down *all* outside rule and authority.

I AM, is the way; I AM, is the light; I AM is the truth.

23

I AM is *within*. Within is I AM! I AM- know thyself- who are you? When Moses asked the burning bush, *"Who are you"* Spirit answered, *"I AM what I AM!"* In other words, don't put me in a box with a label. Just know that I am.

Then, the pendulum swing of fundamental religion is the "anything goes" church. There is no right or wrong. Christ loves you, and no matter what you do, his blood will cover it. So go ahead and eat, drink and be merry. This religion becomes a place to have your conscience soothed. You go and sing, raise your hands, listen to a pep talk, and leave *feeling* very uplifted and close to God- a sort of intoxication on his love. This good feeling may even last for a while and good works ensue as you strive to be pious. But after a while you slip right back into unhealthy ways of living. You feel alone, and separate from God again. Why? *You are not present*. You are not listening to the *word* of God *within*. Rather, you are depending on a religion or religious people to affirm by their teachings that you are okay. The Word *within*, is not recognized nor adhered to, because the relationship with God *inside* your soul is not cultivated. Instead of allowing the Christ- spirit to teach you, being conscious, church becomes a crutch as you hobble along through life, frustrated at your inability to feel fully satisfied and happy.

So in closing, the lie of religion *is* religion; it is systems set up that take the focus off the inner kingdom of God and place it on preaching, practice and dogma. Religious systems have basically conditioned society to believe that God must be sought somewhere without, in some church or among some right group of people. When all the while Jesus, as well as many others, have strived to steer us back to the source of life *within*. Christ awareness brings us that close!

Exercise:

1. If you are currently going to church, ask yourself, "Why do I go to this church/ churches?" Sit somewhere quietly with your journal and really do a soul search. Write down everything that comes to mind. The possibility of reasons is endless. (If you do not go to church, but used to, think about why you used to go. Otherwise, skip the exercise and move on to exercise 2)

Next divide the list under two headings;

a) Unhealthy Reasons

Examples:

- To feel like I belong somewhere
- To find God
- Because I am scared if I don't God will get angry with me and punish me
- Because my family and or friends expects me to go
- Because it makes me feel like I am right with God

b) Healthy Reasons

Examples:

- To fellowship with other believers
- To find friendship
- To find a godly companion
- To praise and worship
- To hear an uplifting message
- To offer my services

You probably will have a mix of healthy and unhealthy reasons. Do the healthy reasons outweigh the unhealthy? Are the healthy reasons you go to church, being met at the church you are attending?

2. Find a quiet place out in nature to be alone for a while. Take your journal and a pen to write. Sit quietly and still your mind of all the racing thoughts. Just set them aside for a while. Become acutely aware of your surroundings- the wind, rustling through the trees and dancing upon the grasses- the birds flittering in the glistening sunlight. Notice the sounds, smells, colors, temperature- all of life all around you- let it all penetrate your soul and become awakened to the presence of God- Know that it takes the breath of God to give life and movement to all that you see and feel. It is the spirit of God that moves you. God is the essence of everything around you. Once you feel truly connected- one with God's essence within and without, take your pen and journal and write to God from *within*. Tell him how you feel; tell him all that is in your heart. Be brutally honest.

After you have poured out your heart to him, sit still and listen within- not with ears, but with awareness. Just listen and write what spirit is saying back to you. Be sure to date your journal. Let this be the beginning of your personal awakening.

Chapter 3

Detoxing From Religion

"At any moment we have two options; to step forward into growth, or to step back into safety."

-Abraham Maslow

"And there came one of the seven angels which had the seven vials, and talked with me, saying to me, Come here; I will show you the judgment of the great whore that sits upon many waters: With whom the kings of the earth have committed fornication, and the inhabitants of the earth have become drunk with the wine of her fornication. So he carried me away in the spirit into the wilderness: and I saw a woman sitting upon a scarlet colored beast, full of names of blasphemy, having seven heads and ten horns. And the woman was arrayed in purple and scarlet color, and decked with gold and precious stones and pearls, and she had a golden cup in her hand full of abominations and the filthiness of her fornication: And upon her forehead was a name written, MYSTERY, BABYLON THE GREAT, and THE MOTHER OF HARLOTS AND ABOMINATIONS OF THE EARTH." Revelations 17: 1-5

Babylon has been said to be spiritual representation of religious organizations that claim to be the bride of Christ, yet they commit spiritual fornication- they are not faithful to Christ's word. This depicts her as arraying herself in purple and scarlet which represents royalty. You will find these colors used in the clothing of the high priest. (Exodus 28) She believes she has spiritual authority. She has a cup of wine in her hand that the "inhabitants of the earth" are intoxicated by.

"And I saw a woman drunken of the blood of saints, and of the blood of the martyrs of Jesus. And when I saw her, I wondered with great wondering." (Revelations 17:6)

We know historically that *religious systems* have been guilty of the bloodshed of countless souls. Also she decked herself with gold, precious stones and pearls which are a biblical depiction the beautiful treasures of God. Religious systems can be very eloquent as they preach their message. Many testify or cast their pearls, to the greatness of their religious system. And so many people have become intoxicated on religious wine.

What exactly happens when one begins to sip on intoxicating drink? Experts have broken the process down into six stages- beginning with just a few sips. See if you can identify any of these with people who become proselyted into a particular religious sect.

Stage 1- Euphoria

Exaggerated happiness; sometimes leading to overconfidence.

Difficulty concentrating; Talkative; Lowered inhibitions

Stage 2- Excitement

Senses are dulled; Poor coordination; Drowsy; Beginnings of erratic behavior;

Slow reaction time; impaired judgment

(When someone begins to sip on religious teachings, the first thing they feel is euphoric. They believe they have stumbled on something special and freeing. They may talk excitedly about it. They will not readily listen attentively to anything you have to say. *Their own inner voice becomes dull* and their judgment becomes erratic)

Stage 3- Confusion

Exaggerated emotions; Difficulty walking; Blurred vision; Slurred speech; Pain is dulled.

(Some church services have great displays of emotional crying and/or shouting. Some even fall on the ground and do all sorts of crazy things. Their speech often ceases to make sense to others. Many lose their ability to walk the journey of life without assistance. Deep emotional issues are ignored and numbed out)

Stage 4- Stupor

Cannot stand or walk; Vomiting; Decreased response to stimuli; Apathetic

(Religion can eventually cause you to become dependent upon their system. You can no longer stand on your own two feet or walk straight without them. You may become spiritually sick and lose touch with reality. The system becomes your reality. After a while, apathy may begin to set in.

Stage 5- Coma

Unconscious; Low body temperature; Possible death

Stage 6- Death

Death as a result of respiratory arrest

(You see this regularly with people who have been in a religion for several years. Their heart is no longer in it. They are like a puppet, going through the motions. Any love and zeal left, it is solely for the system. Personal life in Christ is missing.)

Even a little intoxication can cause you to lose your good judgment. You may begin to feel high and so want to drink more of their religious ideas and beliefs. Your personal inner voice of truth in your heart begins to blur and your ability to hear Spirit's voice within becomes dull, until one day you enter into a complete comatose state where you cannot even perceive what is happening to you; You feel may depressed and anxious, yet put on a happy face. There may be nagging feeling that something is missing within- something very important, but you push it down and keep listening to the institution and the religious beliefs they have indoctrinated you with. By this time, you are too fearful to do otherwise. Eventually, you will spiritually die- you will no longer sense that connection with God.

When it comes to alcohol, there are those who love it, and those who hate it. Among those who love it, there are very few that can utilize just enough for the healthful, helpful, and even enjoyable benefits, and there are those who cannot handle it. It is the same with religion. Religion is like an intoxicating drug. In the right circumstances and with a sober frame of mind, and used for the right purpose, it can be helpful. But it can also be *very dangerous.*

Christ came to turn our hearts back to God. Jesus came to teach us how to reconnect with God. For those of us who believed that God could never love us because we were too guilt-ridden, Christ paid the required penalty. He became the spotless Lamb of God, which takes away the sin of the world. (John 1:29) The sin of the world is rejection of God within. It is to reject the leading of God's spirit within your own beautiful soul and to exchange it for an outside system that sets up dogma and protocol. It is to place our trust in something in the world, rather than in God himself, to guide us through this life. Ultimately, it is the path to death, because when we are not aligned with God within, our authentic-self dies and a shell of diplomacy replaces it. Your beautiful soul is lost in the abyss.

If you recognize that you have already come to this intoxicated state of religiosity, and you desire to be free, there are steps to take in order to detox from religion, so you can begin to hear the true voice of God within your own soul.

1. Take time away- a good long time away from *all* religion. This step, by itself will be very telling, as you will go through religious *withdrawals.* Just like anyone who is sobering up from a drug addiction, at first it will feel very freeing, but then withdrawal symptoms begin to set in. You may experience:

*restlessness
*anxiety
*disturbed sleep patterns
*poor concentration
*depression
*social isolation

Depending on how severe these symptoms are you may want to seek out someone neutral to talk with. A good therapist is helpful; seek out a support group. There are also on-line groups for people coming out of religion.

2. Meditate- clear your mind. Our minds have been so conditioned from the time we came into this world, by religion, culture, media and life-experiences. In the book of Psalms 46:10 it is written, *"Be still and know that I am God."* It is only when we quiet our mind and heart that we will begin to discern the voice of God within. If you are like me, you have a very busy mind, and the thought of quieting it may sound extremely daunting to say the least. I once believed it was impossible for my mind to ever be completely still. I started practicing meditation and I did learn how to still my mind; the results have been phenomenal. There are so many YouTube videos that teach meditation. I found a very simple meditation for myself that has worked wonders. I will be discussing this further in chapter

6. Also, turn off your TV and radio for a while. All that noise and business keeps us from being able to be still and hear the voice of God. I try to be still and have talks with Spirit while I am driving, rather than have the radio blasting.

3. Breaking Free- After you have begun to step away from religion, and to clear your mind, you will begin to have some pretty radical paradigm shifts. As you strive to take these first two steps, you will become *acutely aware of your chains.* This is the place where great courage is called upon. Christ within, has the key to unlock every chain you're bound with:

"Is not this the fast that I have chosen? To loose the bands of wickedness, to undo the heavy burdens, and to let the oppressed go free, and that you break every yoke?" Isaiah 58:6

It will take prayer, meditation, trust, and courage to completely break free. This will not happen overnight. Personal perseverance will be called upon. But it is an amazing journey well worth the effort.

4. Overcoming Denial- One of the most problematic stages of any paradigm shift out there is what is often termed the *denial-system.* Denial works in all of us at some level in life. Denial is a defense mechanism that keeps us from dealing with painful reality. Denying some things gives us a sense of safety. When the walls of denial begin to shatter, our entire world is rocked, and fears and insecurities can overwhelm us and even completely disable us. But to really grow and be completely set free, we must be honest about what *is.* One fact of life that no one can deny is- we are going to die. At some point, each one of us is going to leave this world and everything we love here will be left behind. Most people's denial-system is not shattered until they or a close loved one is at the point of death. It is then that reality has no cloak and for many it is too late to do anything about it.

32

Denial begins at the pivotal point of shutting down your own inner-voice, and allowing another voice to take over. There are many forms of denial. Some deny their children are being abused; some deny that they were abused by a parent, when the evidence is so blatant to others. Some deny they have a drinking or drug addiction. Some deny that their spouse is cheating on them even though their gut is telling them otherwise. Some people deny they have health issues that need to be addressed. The list could go on endlessly. There is a HUGE denial system among the religious world. The denial system in religion is probably one of the most powerful there is to contend with. People continually deny obvious evidence and even facts that disprove the basis of their religious beliefs, because to do so would shake their entire worldview and completely disarm them. Breaking free from denial takes brutal honesty, humility, and a deep hungering desire for full and complete soul freedom. Its takes realizing you're authentic self is being obliterated in a world of fear and deceit. It takes being 100% committed to authenticity!

5. Grief- Once denial is broken, grief usually follows. Grief comes whenever someone suffers a great loss, and it is a loss when we realize our reality was not what we had thought it was. It is important to allow the grief to flow through and express itself and to process what is happening. Again, journaling can be very helpful as well as someone to talk to. The grief does eventually subside. The time it takes is different for everyone. Try to remember that although you are losing one aspect of yourself, you are gaining much more. On the other side of the grief is authentic, soul-freedom and self-expression. On the other side of this process is a settled peace that nothing in this world can ever take away- the peace of knowing, that *God is within and will never leave*- no matter what! God is here to stay when we turn our hearts within.

Chapter 4

Was I the Only One?

"The moment you feel like you have to prove your worth to someone, is the moment to absolutely and utterly walk away."

-Alysia Harris

"TO THE UNKNOWN GOD, Whom therefore you ignorantly worship, I declare him to you. God that made the world and all things in it, seeing that he is Lord of heaven and earth, does not dwell in temples made with hands; Neither is he worshipped with men's hands, as though he needed anything, seeing he gives to all life, and breath, and all things; And has made of one blood all nations of men to dwell on all the face of the earth, and has determined the times before appointed, and the bounds of their habitation; That they should seek the Lord, if haply they might feel after him, and find him, though he is not far from every one of us: For in him we live, and move, and have our being; as certain also of your own poets have said, For we are also his offspring." (Acts 17:23-28)

Reread the scriptures above, slowly and methodically. Wow! Christ told us that, *"the kingdom of God is within you."* Paul told us that God is not found in temples nor worshipped with *men's hands.* Christ told the woman at the well, that God is seeking those who will worship him in *spirit* and in *truth.* So many people wholeheartedly agree with this, yet why do they continue to look for God in temples or churches? They look to religious systems to assure their souls and fulfill their spiritual needs and as they do, so many become caged in the strongholds of religious divisions- or may I go so far as to say, religious insanity. Lies, lies, lies and more lies, spewed out of so many pulpits in the name of Christianity, binding people to all sorts of religious forms, laws, rituals, dogma, and politics until they can no longer even recognize the true voice of Christ inside their hearts.

I understand this from personal experience. Having begun my walk *with Christ alone,* listening to his voice within my heart, I sought earnestly for a "church" or a fellowship of people whom I could worship and serve God with. I had been raised in a fanatical religious cult and so I was doing my best to be so careful about where I set my stakes down. I diligently studied my Bible so no one could "pull the wool over my eyes." I believed that the only natural thing to do when one loves God was to be faithful to going to church- the *right* church that is. I hopped from church to church seeking a place to call my home. Finally, at the age of 27, I found a religious body that seemed to be faithful to the Bible, and to love God with all their hearts. The church services were lively without being strange; everyone seemed to be happily serving. I was so ecstatic, and I mistook my ecstasy for divine enlightenment that these were the *true* people of God. I was so excited to have finally found what I had been searching so long for and I zealously went about telling everyone about "God's true church" and how I had learned there, that we can live "free from sin."

"New truth" was revealed to me and I felt as if my eyes had been opened and God had filled me with divine light. *"Keep coming to church; don't miss anytime the doors are open. Be there,"* was their mantra. *"God has brought you to the glorious, victorious, conquering Church of God. You are privileged. You must have an honest heart. You are among the best people in the world."* On and on, I was pumped up and encouraged and drawn into a new family of God. *"Be careful who you hang around. People are going to fight against the truth. Some will think you are in a cult because you have had such a profound change in your life. Be careful because the devil wants to steal your heart back and take away what God has given you."*

I gave up everything I was told to. "Worldliness" was to be replaced with holiness; worldly music, entertainments, family and friends all must be forsaken. The "holy standard of God," was constantly preached and little by little, I gave up my makeup, grew out my bangs, and exchanged my pants for skirts. I crossed every "t" and dotted every "i" as I was told to. I was zealous. This was it. I had found it and I was not going to ever let it go.

But something very subtle, almost imperceptible began to happen to my faith as I continued on with this church. An intense fear of losing my salvation began to replace the confidence I once had in God. The pure joy I had in knowing Christ's unconditional love was slowly being replaced with sporadic bouts of fear and doubt, all depending on how my performance had been for the day. *"God's love is not unconditional,"* they preached. *"The Bible does not support that."* The church "standard" which they claimed to be biblical applications of holiness, became rules, which if broken, meant certain wrath from both pulpit and the heavenly authority that backed it. And finally, the freedom and elation of serving my Savior became a cage with invisible locks and chains- I no longer felt the freedom within to go out and tell the world about this beautiful Christ that loved them so much and wanted to help them. That now came with a huge price. *"BRING THEM HITHER AND LOCK THEM UP"* was what echoed through my soul when we were admonished to get out there and evangelize with a soul burden.

For the most part, the people were good and sincere and showed kindness and love the best they knew how. I felt like I belonged and had a new family. I felt safe, believing that being a part of this church set me apart for God's special protection. The "standard" was just a small price to pay to know that you are "right with God." These were the chants I regularly heard, heeded and even testified publicly to.

For 18 years I rode an unending roller coaster of spiritual highs and tormenting lows. "You should have a 'know-so' religion!" many would cry out in the services. But I never felt like I knew for sure. Always I feared that one, wrong, fateful slip and God's great mercy would be pulled out from under me and I would be cast into eternal hell fires. I always believed that this was just part of my spiritual battle against the evil one, or what the ministry termed, "the enemy of our souls." So many others from this church had this same internal battle going on too. We just had to "fight the good fight of faith." It was such an oxymoron to hear the choir sing about the battle being over and won through Christ, and then the preacher shout at us that we are in a battle. I felt like I could never really get my bearings. Yes, doctrinally I had it down pat. I wrote tracts and articles to defend my beliefs. But inside I was never fully at peace.

By age 40, I noticed that I was becoming more and more depressed. This was really out of character for me, because I have always been an upbeat person. But I just could not shake this dark cloud that was slowly enveloping my entire existence. I had lost my zeal for Christ- at least for bringing people to church. I knew in my heart I loved God and I did not desire "sinful" things. I could not figure out what was wrong with me.

Then, my family went on a trip to Montana to take part in a series of revival meetings with a congregation we fellowshipped with. While I was there, something preached over the pulpit dumped me in a heap of guilt once again. I made my way down to the altar amongst these strange people and unfamiliar surroundings. A "brother" from our congregation, that had been a constant help to me over the years, knelt next to me and asked if I needed anything. Suddenly, I felt as if a dam broke inside of me that I was not even aware of. I could not stop crying. I kept repeating, *"I wish I had a dad that loved me."* This took me by surprise, because I did not realize that my childhood, darkly shrouded in abuse at the hands of an alcoholic father, was still troubling me that much. The brother did his best to comfort and pray with me, but I continued to cry through most of the night and the following day as well.

After we went home and settled back into our routines, I began having nightmares about my childhood. And so, I naturally blamed my depression on this. I believed that my depression was solely the result of unhealed childhood trauma. The following four years I dove headlong into an agonizing, heart-wrenching, soul-wracking healing process from childhood abuse. The man who helped me at the Montana meeting agreed to help me through this process and really did his best to be there for me. I grew so much and made great strides at improving my low self-view. But oddly enough, the depression did not alleviate- in fact, it grew steadily worse. A few people at church did their best to help, but the reality was, they were not equipped to help. My depression became so severe that I began thinking about ways to end my life. At last I came up with a plan where I could end it in a way that would look like an accident so no one would be traumatized by thinking I had killed myself. I even had reasoned myself into believing God was okay with it. But there was one thing that put the brakes on this thought process- my special-needs daughter. I knew if I died it would devastate her. I was so close to carrying out my plans that I became scared. I contacted a suicide hot-line and got through that very low point. However, the suicidal thoughts were unrelenting.

Then, the man who had been helping me had a life shift and was no longer available to help me. Even when I was able to talk to him, he was so different and aloof. Where his words and empathy once were such a balm for my wounded heart, they were now disconnected and full of religious jargon. I had tied an emotional umbilical cord to this man and losing his support completely shook me to the core. It was like a death blow. I went around in a daze for weeks, not just because of the support being taken away, but also because my entire paradigm was shifting. Something broke inside of me. It was as if I had been under a spell for the past 18 years and suddenly the spell was broken. I saw this church I had been a part of, for the first time, as it *really* was. It was as if I had been drunk all those years and I had suddenly sobered up. I saw that they were just another church among churches- just another religion, casting its net, gathering in souls and locking them into their system of beliefs. And I could clearly see that the strongest chain that held me captive to it was FEAR!

I began to see things that I believe I had always seen, but the "spell" kept from my awareness. For one, the people there were not *really* happy. They were brainwashed; four days a week they all marched to the drumbeat of that message. This did not include all the extra "special" meetings held throughout the year, with visiting pastors and such. One of the first things that is drilled into you when you are converted is that you need to attend every service possible. Every time the doors are open, as far as possible, BE THERE! If you do not show, they call and find out where you are. This is the first place that fear is injected in you; you are told that if you do not come to every service, the enemy will steal you away again. Having now a faithful follower that comes four times a week, the message can be drilled into their brain consistently. Fear is like a spider's venom. She stings her victim into a wakeful paralysis and then begins to weave her webs around and around him so she can drink his life's blood. Her victims are caught in the webs she so cunningly weaves- sticky webs that catch and immobilize you.

The services were like rallies, with people jumping up and shouting their "victory" over sin and the world and the devil. They rallied each other on in their belief system- a sort of spiritual high, that, when people were not shouting or jumping at a service, everyone felt sure something was wrong - "sin must be in the camp," - was a common belief for such apathy. If someone began to feel down or depressed, they were quickly made to feel ashamed amongst such a "joyful" people. Messages to "get into the work" and "to go and think about someone else instead of yourself," would be brought to "help" the downcast one. I mean really, how dare you be anything but joyous for all God has done for you? You were a nothing- nobody! Then, God came along and picked you up out of your sinful condition, and *here* he cleaned you up and *here* he placed you. HERE! IN OUR CHURCH IS WHERE GOD BROUGHT YOU AND YOU DARE NOT LEAVE OR YOU ARE GOING TO BE THE SORRIEST SOUL- LOST! LOST! LOST! FOREVER! SEVEN TIMES WORSE THAN YOU EVER WERE BEFORE!

So fear became the invisible lock and key on the doors. *"There are no locks on our doors!"* the pastor would shout over the pulpit from time to time. *"You can leave anytime! BUT- you will lose your soul!"* They had lured me in with their so-called, "gospel truth," and once I was in they locked me in with seemingly insurmountable fears- into their system of rules and regulations that they claimed were only in place to keep us free from sin and the world. I was to humbly submit to the king that was behind the pulpit who, we were often reminded, was God's special anointed to watch over the flock, and you dare not disobey his authority. If one was caught breaking the rules, they were quickly summoned to the pastor's office and given a verbal lashing and then that lashing continued over the pulpit. Though names were not normally called out, unless deemed important, most knew who he was talking about. So we were brainwashed into submitting our very thoughts and conscience over to the man in the pulpit. He knew better than us because he was God's special anointed. The voice of God within was usurped by him. They taught us to pray and read our Bibles and seek answers from God, but if any of our conclusions crossed up the beliefs, rules or regulations of the system, then that just simply meant that we were not sincere enough in our devotion to God- or perhaps not *honest* enough. I find it so ironic how honesty was defined as being true to them (whom they equated being true to God) and yet being untrue to your inner voice, your authentic self. To me it felt *dishonest* to tell people that I did what I did because I love God, when I knew deep down that much of what I did was because they told me I had to in order to stay right with God. And then they told me not to tell people I keep such rules because I was told to. Those little lies that become so obscure, you start to believe them yourself.

They also offered a sense of family and belonging; when you were good, according to their definition of good, you were treated with love and respect. The people really did seem to care and would pray for one another and work toward the common goal of gathering outsiders in from the treacherous life of sin. But for some reason, I could not just be happy or content and I blamed myself mercilessly for not being more "spiritual."

Over time, as I observed the people in the congregation, and took note of the things they would talk about, it became more and more obvious to me that *I was not the only one* who was experiencing all these struggles with their belief system. I had several engaging heart to heart talks with different ones that would confide in me of their confusion about the "standard," and about church splits that had resulted from these issues over man-made rules. There was concern about how different people were treated at times and the way things were held on us. But always, they resigned to the fatalistic systems ways. Why? FEAR! Intense fear of what might happen if they bucked up or even left. There would be the shunning from all your family and friends and the shame they pronounce on the "backslider" who would be so selfish as to forsake Christ. And then there was the danger of the "enemy" or the devil destroying you without. After all, when you are reminded week after week of how wretched you used to be and how it was all because of this institution you are now a part of that you are where you are today, and if you leave you will be seven times worse than before you came; and when you die, you will burn in a tormenting hell forever and ever. WOW! Who wouldn't fear that! There is no way out. You might as well resign yourself, like it or not! The alternative is far worse.

This no-way-out system of belief was the underpinning of my intense depression. I did not recognize that to begin with. I thought my depression all stemmed from my childhood. But even in childhood, and as a youth, when in the thick of it all, I had never been suicidal to that degree. Depression is caused when who you are at your very core, is *pressed*-down or **de**pressed. Suicide comes from a place of depression- **not allowed to be**. The church became a catalyst to that wounded child within that had never been healed. The ministry tried to help me, but by the very basis on which they operated, they only served to worsen my internal anguish.

One day, during this awakening I was having, God gave me a vision; I saw myself in a large cage, curled up in a ball on the floor, crying and miserable inside this cage, yet the door was wide open. I could leave anytime. But what was keeping me inside the cage was FEAR! I knew I could leave, but I had been told that a serpent waited outside the cage to devour me. But God was telling me, *"Fly away Liz. You are FREE! You will be okay. I AM is watching over you. I have given you wings. Fly away!"* I was so frightened of the consequences of stepping outside the cage. Years of teaching haunted my mind, *"You think you can make it out there? The enemy is just waiting for you. No one has ever left and prospered. Many never make it back. Many who left cannot hear the voice of God anymore. You are free to leave any time- BUT YOU"LL LOSE YOUR SOUL!"*

I did it anyways! It was the most courageous thing I ever did. The longer I sat under their message, after God had broken the spell, the clearer I could see how manipulative it was. The last day I attended services was on a Sunday. I went to both the morning and evening services- two different messages, delivered by two different people, and both were so loaded with fear and woe. One of them was given by the very man who had at one time helped me through some of my darkest hours. I knew after that last service I would never go back. With the help of God, and to the dismay of those that were still in the cage, I spread my wings, and flew away- and God set me FREE!

No matter what a person does, other than line up with whatever the system deems right, you are considered lost. They preach to the congregation about those that leave and use them as examples. *"No one ever leaves and prospers,"* they say. *"See how worldly they have become? See the bad spirit they picked up? They lost all their sweetness. They have drunk from the bitter waters and are defiled."* Nothing and I mean NOTHING a person does or does not do when they leave, is right in their eyes. If they go to another church, that is because they are doubly deceived and have been possessed by a "religious spirit." If they quit dressing the way the church dictates it is because they are immodest and just want the world. The fact is, many that do leave run hard after "sin," because we are told that if we ever leave, we would be better off just going back into sin than getting a "religious" spirit. They have set it up as a no-way-out deal. *It's either our way or the highway, and if you take the highway-* it will be the highway to a certain torcher in hell. So, no matter what the person that leaves does, good or bad, that soul will never be right in the eyes of that institution, because they left them. Also, they emphasize that hardly anyone that leaves, ever makes it back. They give you the idea that the darkness so engulfs you and sin takes you so quickly and it's hard to ever find your way back.

This teaching is so extreme and toxic, because it isolates the person that might not be doing well in that particular system. It hinders them from ever finding a place where they might thrive. There is so little support for people that leave these types of churches. Many are left alone. They don't have the close family relationships anymore. They were told leave all their "worldly" friends and that the church is their new family and friends. That is the trap and how it is set up. Isolation and feeling alone awaits those that leave. The road to recovery is possible but it can be a long and difficult one.

Now, having been on this side of the fence, I can honestly say that the reason people don't "make it back" has more to do with the utter indifference, the shunning and the gossip after they left; you couldn't pay them enough to go back. You come to realize you were never, ever truly loved for who you were; you are loved because you are part of their system. Once you are no longer one of them, you no longer matter. They think they are showing you love because they "carry a burden for you" that you would go back to them. But even in their prayers they curse you. They pray that God would "make you miserable" and "keep you awake at night" and "not let you find any satisfaction out there in the world" until you come back. This is diabolically against the words of Jesus who taught us to "bless and curse not." Where in God's name do you find Christ praying for anyone's misery? The system is loved; the system is worshipped; and Christ himself has been dethroned.

It's so sad because when a soul finally does get to a breaking point and leaves, their faith and trust in God has been so damaged, it's nearly impossible for them to continue to seek for God. So many of these souls just give up and drift back into the sea of sin. But I am here to say, it need not be so. You can hold onto Christ. *The religious picture you have of him in your head is not accurate*. It has been imposed upon you by the system. It will take time away from them to get rid of this delusion. But don't get rid of Christ in the meantime. Keep praying because that is your life-line and the entire reason Jesus came in the first place- is to reconnect you to GOD, not to a religious system. As you learn to listen for the voice of God within, Christ will revolutionize your entire way of seeing not only God, but life itself- and he will make known to you, the incredible value of your own soul. Christ did not come to take away our life- he came to give us a much more abundant life.

"The thief cometh not, but for to steal, and to kill, and to destroy: I am come that they might have life, and that they might have it more abundantly." (John 10:10)

Christ is our savior, even from the religious system. The bible tells us that Jesus himself "suffered without the gate." In other words, he did not go to church- he was shunned! Church would not accept him or his teachings because he would not submit to their hierarchy. His servitude was to the Father of light alone. What was his mission? To find sheep- scattered sheep, lost sheep and bring them back to God. And he himself became the way by his example and self-sacrifice. Hold onto Christ alone. Let Spirit be the commentator in your heart and soul. He will guide you. He will speak to you in your own personal language. You will *clearly* understand when he speaks to you within. Now that I am free, I have so much to share!

Signs of an Unhealthy Church or System:

- **Hierarchy and Control:** *"But Jesus called them unto him, and said, ye know that the princes of the Gentiles exercise dominion over them, and they that are great exercise authority upon them.* **But it shall not be so among you:***"* (Matthew 20:25-26)

- **Lots of money coming from people who are broke; made to feel bad if you do not contribute:** *"And when they were come to Capernaum, they that received tribute money came to Peter, and said, Does not your master pay tribute? He said, "Yes". And when he came into the house, Jesus prevented him, saying, "What do you think, Simon? Of whom do the kings of the earth take custom or tribute money; of their own children or of strangers?" Peter answered him, "Of strangers." Jesus said to him, "Then are the children free."* (Matthew 17:24-26)

- **Loss of personal identity and rights:** *"The thief does not come, except to steal, and to kill, and to destroy: I am come that they might have life, and that they might have it more abundantly."* (John 10:10)

- **Enforcing of rules that you have no say in:** *"Stand fast therefore in the liberty wherewith Christ has made us free, and be not entangled again with the yoke of bondage."* (Galatians 5:1)

- **Separation from society and loved ones that are not in the system:** *"The Son of man came eating and drinking, and they say, behold a gluttonous man, a winebibber, and a friend of publicans and sinners. But wisdom is justified of her children."* (Matthew 11:19)

- **Censoring – no real freedom of speech or freedom of thought:** *"Wherefore, brethren, covet to prophesy, and forbid not to speak with tongues."* (1 Corinthians 14:39)

- **Special lingo-** Religious garb that people that are not familiar with have no idea what you are talking about: *"So likewise you, unless you speak words that are easily understood, how shall it be known what is spoken? For you shall speak into the air."* (1 Corinthians 14:9)
- **Us against them mentality; outside is unsafe; safety comes from staying in the system:** *"And he sent messengers before his face: and they went, and entered into a village of the Samaritans, to make ready for him. And they did not receive him, because his face was as though he would go to Jerusalem. And when his disciples James and John saw this, they said, Lord, will you have us to command fire to come down from heaven, and consume them, even as Elias did? But he turned, and rebuked them, and said, you know not what manner of spirit you are of. For the Son of man is not come to destroy men's lives, but to save them."* (Luke 9:52-56)
- **Burnout, depression, loss of self-worth:** *"But the fruit of the Spirit is love, joy, peace, longsuffering, gentleness, goodness, faith, Meekness, temperance:"* (Galatians 5:22) *"Do not fear, you are of more value than many sparrows."* (Matthew 10:31)

For more information on cults see: CultHelp.info

?

Chapter 5: Learning Self Trust

The Voice Within

A thousand voices cry without,

And fill your heart and head with doubt;

But the Holy Ghost is found within;

Be still! Be still! And listen to Him

Go inside and shut the door,

And every knock without ignore;

In stillness he'll converse with you;

As friend to friend he'll guide you through

Though others may not understand,

Why you march to a different band;

The way of peace and Joy you've found,

For you now stand on holy ground!

A friend of mine once said to me, *"I always tell people who are looking for a church to attend; before you go to any church, first, go and find a closet and enter into it and shut the door; and there pray to God alone."*

We come into this world dependent on others who, for the most part, have never learned to look within. We see the world, we feel our needs; we process what is going on within, through our emotions. We let them be known. But the outwardly focused world hastily stills the inward voice. *Don't do this and don't do that. It isn't proper. What will people think? That isn't acceptable in our society.* So much deliberate and concentrated effort is put into making us all "socially acceptable." Naturally we end up seeking all our needs and affirmations from *without*. That is where we are trained to be focused and concerned with. All the while, God waits patiently for that soul to *be still*. His spirit continually draws us inward, where the breath of God whispers words saturated with infinite love; for he understands that there, and there alone, we find the peace that surpasses all understanding, contentment in all circumstances, healing for our wounded heart, and unspeakable value!

We must turn our hearts back to the Father, in faith. God sent Christ, which, being interpreted means, *anointed one*. Christ was sent to turn us back to God, to help us to know the essence of God by example and by teaching. Then, through his death, Christ satisfied the Mosaic Law once and for all, so that those bound under the law, could be set free from the law. The Mosaic Law required bloodshed to atone for sins. Sin is a result of separation from God, and separation from God results in sin. God is light and love. Sin breaches light and love. Christ came to heal the breach. He taught us that the kingdom of God is within. We must listen within-listen to God *within*. Herein lies the secret to life.

"Do you not know that you are the temple of God, and that the Spirit of God dwells in you?" (1 Corinthians 3:16)

Christ said, *"The kingdom of God is within you."*

Too many are listening to voices outside themselves, rather than turning to the source of light that dwells in every man. (John

1:9) No man could live without God, for God breathed into man, the breath of life. And so it stands to reason that every man has the essence of God within. But too many are in discordance with God. They are looking for their answers to life without, and all the while, the answers lie within. They are seeking approval from without, when all the while, unconditional love lies within. They are seeking value outside themselves, when all the while, the very one who created them and declared, *"IT IS GOOD!"* is found within.

"For in him we live, and move, and have our being; as certain also of your own poets have said, for we are also his offspring." (Acts 17:28)

Faith and *trust* could almost be synonymous of each other. They are central to an abundant life. When faith and trust is flourishing, our lives are balanced and we experience harmony and openness; but as faith and trust diminishes, helter-skelter enters in. We begin to feel detached, lonely, and out of control. Faith and trust magnetize love, peace, joy, happiness, contentment, rest and vitality; the absence of faith and trust leaves us with despair, depression, hopelessness, sadness, complacency, anger and frustration.

But in what should we place our faith and trust? The first and foremost place may surprise you; it may frighten you; and it may even anger you. But please, read this through. The most important place, and the *first* place you need to put faith and trust is in **yourself.** A-men! Without faith and trust in yourself, all other relationships you have- *including your relationship with God-* will ultimately be fraught with unrest. You may have faith and trust in the other person, but the lack of faith and trust in yourself will ever cause a breach, for *faith and trust must come from within first.*

I know this from first-hand experience. Having been raised by an extremely physically and emotionally abusive father, my faith and trust in me was destroyed before I ever understood what the words meant. Consequently, I lived 45 years of my life struggling in every relationship I had, including my relationship with God. When the rubber met the road, it all came down to trust issues with myself. I did not trust people's love for me, because I could not have faith and trust that I was loveable. Therefore I could not trust people's motives. This lack of trust sabotaged my entire world. It was not until I broke loose from every outside voice and began listening to that inner voice of God, that he began to show me, *"Liz, it's time for you to become your own best friend. You need to learn how to trust yourself- to trust your gut, your decisions, your integrity, your motive and you need to have faith in yourself, that you are and will continue to be an upright person. You need to learn to trust, that even when you see something about yourself that you think is not quite on the up and up, that it is okay. We learn, we correct, we grow; it's all part of life."*

You see, it is imperative that you put your trust and faith in yourself. If you don't, it will emotionally cripple you. You might say your trust is in God, but that trust will only go so far when you believe that God cannot trust you, because you cannot trust yourself.

In our formative years, we develop a sense of self through the eyes of others, primarily, our caretakers. Their view of us, and how they treat us, acts like mirrors in which we see ourselves. Blessed is the child who has caretakers that see their immense value and feel the privilege it is to be given the job to care for him or her. But all too often, our formative years are infiltrated with mirrors that were completely inaccurate, and in some cases, devastating to the child. An example of how someone else's energy can be transferred onto you is given in a childhood memory of mine:

I was about six-years-old and my little brother was about four. He came to me and asked me if I wanted to take a bath with him. Fun was dancing all over his countenance at the prospect, like a child excited to go out swimming, and I naturally consented. We were having a blast in the tub, doing all the silly things kids do in a pool of water. My little brother would duck his head underneath the water, and then up he came with his bleach-blonde hair sticking straight up like a mohawk. I belly laughed over and again, never tiring at how funny it he looked.

Suddenly, an icy cold fear instantly silenced us both, as there in the entranceway the enormous figure of our dad glared down at us. Darkness seemed to engulf the room and a sense of impending doom came over me. *I knew at that moment that I was a very naughty and dirty little girl.*

"Jonathan! Get out of the bathtub!" His deep and commanding voice echoed, and the room began to spin. My little brother got out and was rushed off into another room where within ears distance I could hear the lashing of the belt and his pitiful cries. I shivered as I hurriedly pulled my clothes over my wet body. I wanted to get out of there fast before he returned for me. That is all I remember about that incident. The rest is gone- stored away in some safe corner of long ago nightmares.

For many years, whenever that memory came back to my mind, I remembered that my little brother and I were being dirty and naughty taking a bath together- and that was why we got into trouble. I would inwardly cringe as I thought of what a naughty little girl I had been. It was not until I was in therapy, *in my 40's*, that I went back to that memory with my therapist and I realized, that the words "dirty" and "naughty" had never even crossed my mind until the dark form had appeared in the doorway. My dad had *projected* that mirror or energy onto us little innocent children. We were just playing, and having fun. But I was given a message that day from a very prominent figure in my life- *you are a very naughty and dirty little girl that deserves to be punished.*

This is just one of many incidents that clearly illustrates how other people's projections can give us a very distorted self-view in our formative years. We then grow up thinking this is an accurate picture of who we are, and we cease to have any *self-trust*. As a child, my ability to trust myself- to trust that I had good intentions, to trust that I could make right decisions for my life, was *annihilated* by abuse.

Proper discipline will strengthen your inner guidance system, teaching you how to recognize mistakes, and correct them. It will create a balanced way of life. Correct discipline would tell a young child that to take something that does not belong to them is not right. It will guide the child to correct the error by giving back what he/she took; then it will teach the child proper steps to obtaining the desired object, perhaps through asking or purchasing the item. A mistake was made, corrected and a life lesson was learned.

Abuse, however, bypasses these steps and goes directly to the soul of the child and accuses the child of being *evil* or *bad*. Abuse punishes and shames the child for their bad and evil ways, and forces the child to give back what it took. Abuse leaves the child wounded, believing he is bad at his very core.

There is so much power in each of these messages, it is almost inconceivable. These messages now become the framework of our entire life. Growing up with an unscrupulous message about ourselves distorts our self-image and wreaks havoc in our lives. In order to be set free, it must be recognized as wrong and reversed. A new believable message must come into play that will override the original message.

The Message of Salvation

One of the most beautiful messages ever given to mankind is the message of salvation. The true message of salvation is pure light and love. The message of salvation is both simple and complex; it is rich and deep; it makes one light and sets their spirit free.

As soon as the message of *"you're bad, you're dirty or you're no good"* is passed into our realm of thought, we begin to act on it. There is now within us a life-long struggle; now, instead of mistakes being a platform for learning and growing, they become validation to the poisonous messages, and a complication ensues.

In the story of Adam and Eve, they were given a rule - not to eat of the fruit of the tree of knowledge of good and evil. (Genesis 2:17) No one knows exactly why; many religions speculate that it was to test their love and faithfulness to God. Whatever the reason, the fruit was of the knowledge of good and evil and they were forbidden to partake of it. And when they broke that rule, something happened that day that most all religions agree upon- *they died within*. Death is the opposite of life. Life was taken from them - not physically, but *inside*. You see, they received a new message that day that they did not have beforehand- after they had partook of the fruit, they received another message that they were now bad, dirty and no good. We can see this by their actions that followed. They hid from God and covered their naked bodies so they would not be seen. For the first time, they felt *shame.* They no longer felt like they could be one with God, to walk with him and talk with him. They moved away from love and light and into the dark shadows of guilt and shame.

There was nothing God could do at this point to undo the poisonous message they had taken in. The message had taken root in their hearts and they believed the lie. And so we have the story of the conception of sin- or separation from God.

"For as he thinks in his heart, so is he" (Proverbs 23:7)

The mind is both theoretically and scientifically proven to be so powerful. The belief that at our core we are bad- when we believe this, we will eventually act on it, no matter how much we struggle against it, because it is our *belief about ourselves*. There was an expulsion of Adam and Even out of the Garden of Eden- or the paradise experience of walking and talking with God. And so as time went on, God became separated from man as man viewed God with fear and unworthiness and passed this self-view onto their offspring. As the Biblical stories progress, we find man doing all he can to appease an angry God. He has gone so far as to believe he must be punished for his badness and so begins to find a substitute to avoid his own punishment. He begins to offer animal sacrifice in his place of what he believes he deserves. I do not believe that God ever put forth this practice into the world but rather it came from the fearful mind of man. As man begin to avoid listening to God within, he replaced that voice with superstition and religious practices.

Jesus came as a spiritual master, the offspring of God, to relieve and satisfy the mind of man once and for all, that he was *not* bad, and so could reunite with God. He offered himself- a perfect man- instead of an animal. As a man who had a direct connection with God- the Christ consciousness or anointing of the Spirit- he became a living sacrifice for all men, not just those who were Jews, but for the entire world. He surmounted the barriers of religious systems, put down all religious authority over men and opened the way for them to have the same Christ consciousness as he had- complete trust in the sovereignty of God within all humanity.

The message of salvation is a message of love and light- it is a message to reunite the soul with God- to give the soul the confidence to, once again, walk and talk with God. Jesus taught us where to find God and his kingdom- *within*. The message of salvation is purely to reunite us with God- to turn us from placing all our trust on everyone and everything without- what our eyes see, what our ears hear; it teaches us to turn to our inner guide- his spirit within. God wants us to know we can trust our own inner guide. He wants you to know that he trusts you, and you can have faith and trust in yourself. Light and love is calling from within. Will you heed the call?

Exercises:

1) Take time to write in your journal a list of positives about YOU and identify them with the great and powerful I AM....

I AM trustworthy

I AM a child of God

I AM loveable

I AM beautiful

I AM cherished by God

I AM honorable

I AM honest

I AM pure

Add more to the list. Make it as personal as possible. Take note of any areas of resistance or disbelief in what you are writing. If you write, I am honest, and you feel a struggle, go into the shadow places of your heart, where you may believe something is wrong with you; acknowledge what you have believed and then recognize that it is inaccurate mirror. Be still and let your inner voice of God guide you. Maybe you will see that dishonesty was a distorted mirror placed on you by someone else in your developmental years. Perhaps there were times when you lied to your abusers out of fear. Did that make you a dishonest person? Or was that the only way a helpless little child knew how to protect his/her self?

If you have come to believe certain things about yourself, you very well may be fulfilling them. Let God's gentle spirit walk you through to a place where you can shed the false identity and replace it with what your heart truly desires, "I AM honest." Then, if that inner voice directs you to areas in your current life where you are fulfilling that false message, let it also help you get to the root of why. Remember this is about being immersed in God's Spirit and his spirit will do a thorough work. It is not to shame you- it is to beautify you. It is to rid you of these areas that are blocking the pure energy and vitality of God's beautiful spirit flowing through you. So this may be an area of much prayer and meditation and may take many days, months or even years to work through. For some people, the impact of trauma and abuse has been so severe in their lives, that this process can be excruciatingly painful and difficult to move through. It will require much courage and tenacity. Be gentle with yourself.

2) Start practicing being your own best friend- your own best advocate. Stand up for yourself. Love yourself. Rejoice in the beautiful, uniqueness of your own soul. And above all, TRUST yourself. Friendship demands trust. Say to yourself today, *"Name- I love you! I am your best friend and I got your back!"*

Chapter 6

For the Bible Tells Me So

"Brother, you say there is but one way to worship and serve the Great Spirit. If there is but one religion, why do you white people differ so much about it? Why not all agreed, as you can all read the Book? "

-Sogoyewapha, "Red Jacket"

This question asked years ago by a Native American Indian, still has great relevance today. If the Bible is the infallible word of God, and we all read the same book, why are there so many divisions about the book? I have been a part of several religions throughout my lifetime and they each give a general explanation that somehow the seeker is not earnest enough and that is why they haven't seen it the way "they" see it.

Jesus taught that man should not live on bread alone, but by ***every word that proceeds out of the mouth of God.*** (Matthew 4:4) Let us again consider what he did not say. He did not say, *Man shall not live on bread alone but by every word that is written in the scriptures.* Jesus also told his disciples that he always did those things which please the Father. (John 8:29)

I don't know about you, but I always pictured Jesus as having an on-going conversation with the Father. He heard God within. He listened to God within. He was one with God. *The "word" was within him*, and his mission was to bless us with this same relationship with God. He prayed right before he was to be crucified, *"And the glory which you have given me I have given them; that they may be one, even as we are one:"* (John 17:22)

59

Many scriptures talk about how Jesus went about preaching the "Word" and we know he was not preaching the old law, but he was preaching the "Word" as it was revealed to him. In St. John 1 we read: *"In the beginning was the Word, and the Word was with God, and the Word was God. The same was in the beginning with God. All things were made by him; and without him was not anything made that was made. In him was life;"*

Genesis 1 reads, *"In the beginning God created the heaven and the earth. And the earth was without form and void, and darkness was upon the deep, and the Spirit of God moved upon the waters. And God said, "Let there be light, and there was light. . ."*

God created with his Word; in the beginning was the "Word" and the "Word" was with God; the "Word" *was* God.

The Bible is not the Word; God is the Word, and the Word became flesh; the Word is Christ- or the anointing. For we know that God is a spirit. (John 4:24)

The Bible is a compilation of many books written by "holy men of God" as they were moved by God's spirit. (2 Peter 1:21) I am moved by God's spirit to write this book. It is my passion that it will be used to the greater understanding of who God is, and where we are in relationship to God. But I know that this book is not, nor ever will be all encompassing. I have a limited viewpoint as does every other single person on planet earth. In another place in the Bible it states, *"All scripture is given by inspiration of God, and is profitable for doctrine, for reproof, for correction, for instruction in righteousness:"* (2 Timothy 3:16) But this scripture was written about the Old Testament, for they did not have a New Testament at that time it was written. And the author of Timothy said, "ALL scripture."

What is *all scripture* anyhow? To most, it is all the books that were carefully selected by a panel of men that King James appointed. But most Bible scholars are well aware of the great controversies about what was selected and what was left out and about the discrepancies even within the ones that were left in. Any google search will give you a vast amount of information about these issues. Again, let's consider what Timothy does not say here; He does *not* say, All scripture is given as the WORD of God and it necessary for salvation, for connection to God, and to verify if personal divine revelation is relevant or not.

When it comes to Christianity, the Bible is unparalleled. It is an irreplaceable treasure. The Bible is our sole historical record of Christ Jesus' life, death and resurrection. For the Christian it is a rich source of comfort, strength, truth and guidance. No other written works out there come even close to receiving the reverence and close scrutiny as the Holy Bible. But even so, *the Bible is not the infallible word of God*. There is not even one scripture within the Bible that backs up this belief. It may feel like I am splitting hairs here, but truly, it is because of this one tiny strain at a gnat, that so much of Christianity swallows the camel of hatred, division and seclusion. (Matthew 23:24) Because people worship the Bible as the "infallible word of God," history is bloodied with accounts of merciless, intolerance by those who have thought themselves to be the ambassadors of "truth." *"They will cast you out of the synagogue* (places of worship); *yes, the time will come, when those that kill you will think they are doing the service of God. And they will do these things, because they have not known the Father nor me"* (John 16:2-3) Now tell me something, do you see light and love in this?

The Bible is a *written witness* of men who wrote about their experiences with God or spirit. The apostles were flesh and blood, no different than you and I. The Old Testament Bible, is a compilation of historical records written by what some termed were "Holy men of God;" Likewise the New Testament is a compilation of letters, written by people no different than you and I. The compilation of these letters was done by a group of men. The translations were done by men, no different than you and I. True, they may have been specially chosen for different work, but so are we. What these flesh and blood men and women did was listen to the Word of God within their spirit:

"And it shall come to pass afterward, that I will pour out my spirit upon all flesh; and your sons and your daughters shall prophesy, your old men shall dream dreams, your young men shall see visions: And also upon the servants and upon the handmaids in those days will I pour out my spirit." (Joel 2:28-29)

"This is the covenant that I will make with them after those days, says the Lord; I will put my laws into their hearts, and in their minds will I write them;" (Hebrews 1016)

"But you have received the Holy Spirit, and he lives within you, so you don't need anyone to teach you what is true. For the Spirit teaches you everything you need to know, and what he teaches is true—it is not a lie. So, just as he has taught you, remain in fellowship with Christ." (1 John 2:27)

Every human has within them this natural longing for wholeness- which is alignment with our creator. Perfect alignment is a state of perfect soul satisfaction, peace, harmony, and rest. However, because we have been so used to practicing misalignment, we find ourselves, so much of the time, in a state of dissatisfaction, turmoil and unrest. These feelings disturb us, and so we seek out that perfect alignment. In our "Christian-culture" we have been programmed for generations that the way to perfect alignment or, connections with God is to go to church, and to constantly read and study the Bible, which has been religiously characterized by Christian culture as "the word of God." Therefore, as we read the Bible, whenever we come across scriptures that talks about the "Word", we think of the Bible. But the "Word" is not the Bible.

To become aligned with God is to experience wholeness within. It is to be complete: *"For in Christ lives all the fullness of God in a human body. So you also are complete through your union with Christ"* (Colossians 2: 9 & 10) Once God has cleared the way for us to come to him without fear of rejection, there is a very natural desire to be closer to him and to know him. But our lives that we have lived hitherto have been in discordance with God. And so, this new relationship takes time to grow into perfection. We will still find that there are habits and ways of living that get in the way of oneness with God. This world also provides much distraction. The Bible is therefore *"profitable for doctrine, for reproof, for correction, for instruction in righteousness: That the man of God may be perfect, thoroughly furnished unto all good works."*(2 Timothy 3:16-17) But it was for a relationship with God that Christ died for.

We should never, ever, replace studying the Bible over seeking communion with God. We should never value the written words of the scripture, above the whispered word of God into our hearts. It would be the same as if you got married to someone, and, ignoring your new spouse, you read all about him through cards and letters collected over the years. You carefully study things other people had said about him, and by this you go about trying to figure out how to best please him. But you spend very little time talking and sharing with him. You never asked him to verify or validate, or explain what the things written about him meant. You just took those written witnesses at face value and went about like you knew everything about your spouse. And when your spouse does talk to you, you always go and search the letters to make sure what he is saying is legit. It sounds ludicrous I know, yet this is exactly what we are doing when we dissect the scripture, study it, write it down, memorize it, etc.... all the while spending so little time being still and *listening* to Spirit within.

Most of the early church did not even have access to a Bible. They had to pray and listen for God *within* to be successful in their walk. And those who did not listen within, looked to other men to teach them about God. When that happened, divisions began. As soon as people got away from *listening* and *personal communion* with God, and began looking *without* for their assurance, hierarchy entered and splits began; wars commenced, hatred was fed and blood was spilt; and it has been that way ever since. Beginning in the home, one child no longer believes what his parents teach him. The parents are mortified because they believe what they have been taught *without* is the real *interpretation of the Bible.* Religious strife and division infects every part of this world.

Never, ever, place the discourse of a man that you consider to be close to God, over seeking communion with God. **Listen to God within your own heart.** I cannot stress this enough. It is so imperative. The entire prejudice, judgmental, vicious, religious mess we see out in the world today is due to people placing their trust in things without, rather than on the "WORD" of God **within**. *"We ought to obey God rather than men."* (Acts 5:29)

A personal experience of mine will give a clearer picture of what I am talking about. In the fundamental church I attended, we prided ourselves on knowing and "rightly dividing" the "word of God" -meaning the Bible. We considered ourselves the "true and faithful." Now in the Bible we read to *"Obey them that have the rule over you, and submit yourselves: for they watch for your souls."* (Hebrews 13: 17) And so when a pastor preached, we paid close attention. One of the things I was taught by our pastor was that we do not give unwed mothers baby showers, for that is the same as approving of their sin. Indeed, the Bible tells us, "*Do not be unequally yoked together with unbelievers: for what fellowship has righteousness with unrighteousness? And what communion does light have with darkness?*" (2 Corinthians 6:14) Well, we live in a time and culture when, for a variety of reasons, unwedded mothers are quite the norm. So for me, this was a hard pill to swallow. The time came when I was truly "put to the test." However, by this time, I was well beyond bowing to the voices without and God had been working on me to listen to him alone.

A young girlfriend of my oldest daughter was pregnant and living with a man out of wedlock. In respect of confidentiality I will keep the details out of this account. But this young girl had been through so much heartache and religious confusion. She had so little support, and my daughter and another young lady only 16 at the time, decided to give her a baby shower. I did not say much about it. I figured this was her conviction and I would just let her do what she felt was right. However, my mind was in turmoil. I had been taught, biblically directed, by a much respected pastor, that we don't do this type of thing. Yet I knew this girl needed as much help and support as she could get. Within my heart, I yearned to help her. The day got closer to the date set for the baby shower. I could tell that my daughter and her friend were struggling to pull this together as they had so little money and had never given a shower before. I finally listened to that still small voice within over the loud and aggressively preached word. At the last minute I jumped in and did all I could to help give her a wonderful baby shower.

On the way home from the party, I was in my car, alone, and I was looking out at the beautiful California sunset. I had that warm feeling that only comes from serving someone in need, and yet I was still wondering if I had done the right thing- if I had pleased God or not. Suddenly, I literally felt the spirit of God wrap me up in such a blissful assurance of love and acceptance, and heard within my heart, *"You did good Liz. I am well pleased. You are like your Father in heaven, for He, "makes his sun to rise on the evil and on the good, and sends rain on the just and on the unjust."* (Matthew 5: 45) I had listened to the Word of God within, and the Word within led me straight! Peace and joy ensued.

No two people will ever see the Bible exactly the same because no two people will ever have the exact same perception. No two people will ever be led of God exactly the same because no two people have the exact same position, life experience or purpose. It is virtually impossible. ***To say that everything God shows us within our heart must line up with the Bible is to imprison the soul and disconnect it from the source of life- the Word.*** The Bible is still valuable, and profitable. But it is not the infallible Word. If this was true, then the virgin Mary could never have been overshadowed by the Holy Spirit, Joseph could never have taken a pregnant woman to be his wife, Hosea could never have married a harlot, Abraham would never have offered up Isaac, Peter would have never eaten unclean meat nor accepted the Gentiles into the fold of God and Saul would never have departed from his faith to take on the work of Christ. ***All these were contradictory to the <u>written</u> scripture***. It took the *Word of God- within*, to speak to all those throughout the Bible and it takes the voice of God within to speak to us today, for today we have unique challenges, a different culture and greater knowledge and understanding.

Practice looking to God within- constantly and consistently. Practice quieting your mind and heart. *"Be still and know that I am God."* Practice listening to the voice of God within, hushing all other voices. Detox yourself from religious ideas and just let God speak to your heart for a while. I have had to put aside my Bible for long periods of time, because the meanings behind the scriptures have been so tainted by the religious ideas of our day. *But putting away the scripture is not the same as putting away God.* When this relationship with God is personal, when it is real, when you feel that wholeness, that complete acceptance and unconditional love of God, when you are immersed in his spirit- It is beautiful, lively, and POWERFUL!

The New Testament is letters written to the people of God in various locations, addressing various needs in another culture and time. Sure they can be a benefit, for they are a witness of Christ. We read men's accounts of their relationship with Christ and what they learned of him. But they are *not* the new commandments written in stone for our generation. God said he would give us his *spirit* - he would write his laws on our new, tender hearts. We no longer need harsh tables of stone with commandments pounded out to us. We have a *new spirit* and a *new heart*. Do you believe this? Do you not trust what God has given you? Unfortunately, many do not, and throughout the years so many precious souls have been wounded, caged, whipped and bruised by ignorant pastors believing themselves to be another Moses.

Jesus paid the penalty that the Hebrew law demanded for transgression of the law, once and for all. Thank God for that. Look to Christ Jesus. Look upon the cross. See the sacrifice paid for sins, once and for all. We no longer live under "Thou shalt," and "Thou shalt not." We are FREE! *"Then are the children free."* (Matt. 17:26) We will naturally bear good and holy fruit, because Christ- the anointing is now within. There is now alignment with the Spirit of God. *"For if the first fruit be holy, the lump is also holy: and if the root be holy, so are the branches."* (Romans 11: 16)

And IF we sin, God forbid, but IF we fall, if we become misaligned, praise God, we have an advocate- Jesus Christ the righteous. (1 John 2:1) *"For a just man falls seven times, and rises up again:"* (Prov. 24:16). The Spirit of Christ in us is so wonderful, its love is so beautiful, it's light so glorious, we are naturally repelled by things that are dark and hateful- we have a new and different spirit.

Again, let me stress that this is not to discount the Bible. I am so thankful for the holy record and it is obvious in my writing here that I cherish it and utilize its teachings. My Bible is very well worn. But the Bible is not the New Ten Commandments, written in stone. No! *"The letter kills but the spirit gives life."* (2 Corinthians 3:6)

Within your heart lies the precious Word and that Word knows you very intimately. The Word is very personal to you and is speaking in a still small voice within your soul. The Word will call you by your name. The word will teach you and give you understanding within your heart. (1 John 2:27)

Does that mean we never need to be taught by anyone outside ourselves? Of course not, for if that were true, I would not be writing this book. But the religious world is very imbalanced and for the most part points you to an outward focus rather than and inward communion. The churches or the Bible are not the Word- they were inspired *by* the Word; However, God writes the "Word" on our hearts; It is written there as fresh manna from heaven- day by day, for our own unique situation, time and culture.

The Word of God is keeping us from within- aligned with him!

Challenge:

*Have you ever read books of other faiths? I challenge you to pick one and take work through it. Use a highlighter and mark passages that resonate with you. Write quotes in your journal that are enlightening. Notice when you start to go into all-or-nothing type of thinking as your read, meaning, when you find something you believe is wrong or goes 100% against what you believe, you begin to mentally discredit the entire book. Or when you find a spiritual book extremely enlightening you hallow the entire book or the author.

Challenge yourself to take what resonates with you and leave what doesn't.

Dare to read what you never dared before. Trust yourself, that you have a good heart and that you will choose what is right and good and leave what is dark and unhealthy for you.

Here is a spring board of ideas, but do not limit yourself here. Go to the library and scour the 100's section. Watch you come alive as you begin to feed that curious child within once again. Life is meant to be explored and to learn and to grow!

Autobiography of a Yogi by Paramahansa Yogananda, "is a beautifully written account of an exceptional life and a profound introduction to the ancient science of Yoga and its time-honored tradition of meditation. Profoundly inspiring, it is at the same time vastly entertaining, warmly humorous and filled with extraordinary personages. . . Selected as "One of the 100 Best Spiritual Books of the Twentieth Century", Autobiography of a Yogi has been translated into more than 30 languages, and is regarded worldwide as a classic of religious literature. Several million copies have been sold, and it continues to appear on best-seller lists after more than sixty consecutive years in print."

With engaging candor, eloquence, and wit, Paramahansa Yogananda tells the inspiring chronicle of his life: the experiences of his remarkable childhood, encounters with many saints and sages during his youthful search throughout India for an illumined teacher, ten years of training in the hermitage of a revered yoga master, and the thirty years that he lived and taught in America...The author clearly explains the subtle but definite laws behind both the ordinary events of everyday life and the extraordinary events commonly termed miracles. His absorbing life story becomes the background for a penetrating and unforgettable look at the ultimate mysteries of human existence.

The Untethered Soul by Michael A. Singer, "whether this is your first exploration of inner space, or you've devoted your life to the inward journey, this book will transform your relationship with yourself and the world around you. You'll discover what you can do to put an end to the habitual thoughts and emotions that limit your consciousness. By tapping into traditions of meditation and mindfulness, author and spiritual teacher Michael A. Singer shows how the development of consciousness can enable us all to dwell in the present moment and let go of painful thoughts and memories that keep us from achieving happiness and self-realization."

Bhagavad-Gita: The Song of God by Swami Prabhavananda, "The Bhagavad-Gita is the Gospel of Hinduism, and one of the great religious classics of the world. It's simple, vivid message is a daily inspiration in the lives of millions throughout the world and has been so for countless generations."

A Guide to the Present Moment by Noah Elkrief, "This book will show you how to disbelieve the thoughts that create your unwanted emotions. As soon as you stop believing a thought that is creating one of your unwanted emotions, that emotion will instantly dissolve. As you disbelieve more and more of the thoughts that create your suffering, you will be happier in more and more situations, the more you will be living in the moment, and the more peace, love, laughter, wholeness, enthusiasm, and gratitude you will experience in your life."

The Upanishads: A Classic of Indian Spirituality by Eknath Easwaran, "Among the oldest of India's spiritual texts, the Upanishads are records of intensive question-and-answer sessions given by illumined sages to their students. Widely featured in philosophy courses, the Upanishads have puzzled and inspired wisdom seekers from Yeats to Schopenhauer. Eknath Easwaran makes this challenging text more accessible by selecting the passages most relevant to readers seeking timeless truths today."

Journey of Souls: Case Studies of Life between Lives by Michael Newton, "Learn the latest details and most recent groundbreaking discoveries that reveal, for the first time, the mystery of life in the spirit world after death on Earth—proof that our consciousness survives... Journey of Souls is a graphic record or "travel log" by these people of what happens between lives on Earth. They give specific details as they movingly describe their astounding experiences.

After reading Journey of Souls, you will gain a better understanding of the immortality of the human soul. You will meet day-to-day challenges with a greater sense of purpose. You will begin to understand the reasons behind events in your own life.

Journey of Souls is a life-changing book. Already, over 165,000 people have taken Journey of Souls to heart, giving them hope in trying times. You should read a copy, too.

The Heart of the Buddha's Teaching: Transforming Suffering into Peace, Joy, and Liberation by Thich Nhat Hanh, "Covering such significant teachings as the Four Noble Truths, the Noble Eightfold Path, the Three Doors of Liberation, the Three Dharma Seals, and the Seven Factors of Awakening, The Heart of the Buddha's Teaching is a radiant beacon on Buddhist thought for the initiated and uninitiated alike."

Gandhi: An Autobiography - The Story of My Experiments with Truth, "Mohandas K. Gandhi is one of the most inspiring figures of our time. In his classic autobiography he recounts the story of his life and how he developed his concept of active nonviolent resistance, which propelled the Indian struggle for independence and countless other nonviolent struggles of the twentieth century."

No Greater Love by Mother Teresa, "the essential wisdom of Mother Teresa — the most accessible, intimate, and inspiring book of her teachings. Thematically arranged to present her revolutionary vision of Christianity in its graceful simplicity, the book features her thoughts on love, generosity, forgiveness, prayer, service, and what it means to be a Christian. A passionate testament to deep hope and abiding faith in God, No Greater Love celebrates the life and work of one of the world's most revered spiritual teachers."

*Book details borrowed from Amazon.com

Chapter 7

Prayer is Immersion into God

"A quiet mind is able to hear intuition over fear."

"And when you pray, do not be as the hypocrites are: for they love to pray standing in the synagogues and in the corners of the streets, that they may be seen of men. Truly I say to you, they have their reward. But you, when you pray, enter into your closet, and when you have shut the door, pray to your Father which is in secret; and your Father which sees in secret shall reward you openly." (Matthew 6:5-6)

The Secret Closet- here lays the essence of this entire book. The secret closet is a place within your soul; it is that holy ground that no one else can enter, unless you open the door of your soul up to them. But God says, enter in, and shut the door, so that you and I can commune *alone*. The key here is *going within-* with God-alone! Everything outside is shut out and left outside. The voice you commune with and allow to lead your life is shut within the closet of your precious soul. Although time alone and space alone is crucial, this is not what it is referring too. It is referring to that holy ground *within* that is not exploited to the ravages of the outer world. This closet of your own soul goes with you wherever you go.

For years I had a certain form of prayer; I knelt on my knees, bowed my head, closed my eyes and began speaking to God. Through much practice and study, I learned to begin with thanksgiving, and then I delved into all the woes and concerns and "laid it all at his feet." When I went through my deepest depression in my early forties, I nearly always began my prayer crying. No sooner did I hit my knees, when a flood of tears would rush out from deep inside. My heart was so broken; sometimes I would never even speak a word. But it was at those times that I felt the spirit of God with me closer than ever. Later on, after I left the church I had been attending for so many years, I realized that the Bible never really gives a specific form that we are to take when we pray. I had been studying a little about the benefits of mediation and I began to change my form or prayer to sitting in a crossed legged position on my couch, early in the morning while I was alone, in traditional meditation form, I would practice quieting my mind. This is the main discipline of meditation- to completely quiet the mind from all the thoughts racing through it. In the beginning, it was very difficult for me. I am a deep thinker by nature and to actually still my thoughts was not easy. But I read a lot of tips online. I learned to concentrate on the empty spaces between thoughts and practice making those spaces bigger. So each time I would find an empty space in my mind, with no thoughts, it was my discipline to hold that space for as long as possible, allowing the space to grow larger.

As I practiced quieting and clearing my mind, my prayer life was enriched, and the voice of God became so much clearer to me. I turned my focus inward, and then I would visualize all the blessings I had surrounding my life and one by one I would give thanks from within my heart- *I entered into a state of gratitude.* My prayer life shifted from me doing a lot of talking, asking, and pleading to entering into stillness, gratitude, enlightenment, acceptance and positive vision. Instead of pleading for others, I began visualizing, from a prayerful heart, the positive outcome I desired for them. So, if someone was sick, I would visualize them as being healthy and whole as a prayer rose up from within my heart that it might be so. My prayer life shifted from me being immersed in my cares and concerns, doubts and fears, worries and problems, to me being immersed in Spirit!

"Be still and know that I am God." (Psalms 46:10) There is a lot of power in this statement. If you doubt that, I challenge you to write it down on several slips of paper and place it all over your home. Repeat it to yourself as often as you think of it- *"BE STILL, and KNOW that I AM GOD!"* When you become still before God, and immersed into Spirit, something very beautiful begins to unfold. You crawl your way within as if entering into a cocoon, but when you come out, you are changed into a beautiful butterfly with wings.

You see, this cannot happen by just going to church; when our trust and hope is placed in the system that we believe is "God's church," we will crawl in like a caterpillar and come back out feeling like a worm. Many times we feel changed alright, and humbled, but definitely not beautiful and precious nor free, flying from flower to flower sipping sweet nectar. Rather, we laboriously are crawling up prickly stems and gnawing on the leaves. We are still on the ground feeling more challenged than ever to reach the place of clear vision, sweetness of life and soul freedom.

Prayer is communion with our creator. I will repeat, PRAYER is *communion* with our CREATOR- the one who *created* YOU! Awesome thought! Prayer is not just a conversation with God. It's a communication that embodies perfect oneness. Prayer is a quieting of the mind of all life's distractions and unclogging the flow of God's energy through our lives.

There is a scripture that teaches us to *"pray without ceasing."* (1 Thess. 5:17) - it basically says to never stop praying! This would seem like a pretty tall order if you are thinking of prayer in a traditional 'Christianized' sense- in the way churches typically present prayer to God. But when you begin practicing *meditative* prayer- quieting the mind, and allowing God's energy (or spirit) to freely flow through you, this becomes a natural way of life- it becomes a prayer that never ceases.

Many Christians become alarmed at terms such as meditation, God's energy and looking within. They immediately jump to the judgment that it is just mixing eastern religion with Christianity. However, becoming alarmed just validates the fact that churches have boxed up religion into such a form, that a soul can no longer expand, grow, and allow the Holy Spirit to enlighten them to greater heights in God.

Take a moment to read Acts 10:9-10.

We read that the apostle Peter went up to pray, and fell into a *trance*, and saw a vision from God. The Bible does not describe the form Peter was in, because that is irrelevant. But he fell into a trance- *a meditative state of mind*, and in this state, God communicated something to him. What he communicated was something *very new* to Peter; He told him to do something that, back then, to the church of his time, was considered a BIG no! No! He told Peter to eat animals that were *unclean*. This, my friend, was completely unscriptural. Even Peter exclaimed to God, "Not so Lord!" He was not about to go against the Bible. But it didn't stop there. God went on to tell Peter to do something that was even a greater no! No! Peter was to receive the Gentiles as God's people too. He was to offer salvation in Christ and equality to every man in every nation. This was BIG NEWS- and really, what could cause a greater ripple in the already growing currents with the Jews? And to think that Peter received this message from God, while in a "trance"- praying!

God wants us to become immersed in his Holy Spirit- the Bible describes it as being baptized with the Holy Spirit. When that happens, something very beautiful and glorious transpires- your spirit becomes one with God's spirit. This is the fullness of reconciliation to God. This is the desire of God's heart. This was the purpose of Christ's sufferings. It was not to create a "church" as we have come to understand it in our modern way of thinking. It was to show you the beauty and value of your own soul, and the only way you can ever truly see that, is when your spirit is immersed completely in God, and God alone! Not immersed in church, or in a doctrine, not in a creed or a certain discipline of life, not in a teaching, not in a group of people, not in a school of thought, not in a book, not even in the Bible- but in Spirit! All these other things listed here, should only serve to point and prod you toward your personal and intimate experience with God. None of them should lay claim of access to God, for there is only one access and that is the anointing- the Christ spirit.

In the secret closet of your soul, you can talk with God about whatever may be troubling you. If you have done something wrong, talk to God about it. If you are hurt, angry, confused, scared, sad, lonely, unbelieving, or even suicidal- tell God alone. Be still and listen for his still small voice within your soul. It may be difficult at first to decipher between the spirits voice and all the noise in your head. But ask God to help you recognized Spirit's voice within. Ask him for the cleansing and anointing of Christ.

"A new heart also will I give you, and a new spirit will I put within you: and I will take away the stony heart out of your flesh, and I will give you a heart of flesh." Ezekiel 36:26

With Christ in that sacred place within, YOU are the "church" or the "temple" of God.

"God that made the world and all things therein, seeing that he is Lord of heaven and earth, dwells not in temples made with hands;" Acts 17:24

"And what agreement has the temple of God with idols? For you are the temple of the living God; as God has said, I will dwell in them, and walk in them; and I will be their God, and they shall be my people." 2 Corinthians 6:16

Return often to that sacred and quiet place "within" and listen to the voice of God. He will meet you as friend to friend. Ask him to immerse your soul completely, to baptize you, to pour out his spirit on you as the Bible said he would. Ask him to help you *clearly discern* Spirit's voice apart from all others. God will honor this request because he loves you- because this is the desire of God's heart- because in the eyes of God, your soul is beautiful and valuable.

Exercise

1)   Another exercise I have found that helps to lift me within to a space of gratitude is to be still. Close your eyes and relax your body as much as you can, breathing in deeply. Then listen and find what your ears may pick up that is relaxing, that makes you feel safe and happy inside. Then, slowly open your eyes, and again find anything within your immediate surroundings that feels comforting to you and enter into those comforting feelings. This exercise will bring you into a space of serenity and make it easier to enter into a space of gratitude.

2)   Try practicing mediation. I have a short YouTube video available that you will find on my blog: http://fortysixplus.blogspot.com/Just click on the right, under the tab "Labels" - "meditation."

3)   Write the words, "Be still and Know that I am God," on several sticky notes and hang them all over the house, in your car. Place them wherever you will see them often. Say the words aloud to yourself. Let their deep meaning sink into your soul until it feels as if a light switch goes on inside and you are seeing God as you have never seen him before.

Chapter 8

Dethroning the Mighty Pastor

"At that time the disciples came to Jesus and asked, 'Who, then, is the greatest in the kingdom of heaven?' And Jesus called a little child to him and placed the child among them. And he said: 'Truly I tell you, unless you change and become like little children, you will never enter the kingdom of heaven. Therefore, whoever takes the lowly position of this child is the greatest in the kingdom of heaven. And whoever welcomes one such child in my name welcomes me." (Matthew 18:1-5)

Little children love to learn. They are curious and easy to influence. Life is always in the moment for them, and each new experience an adventure. They are not concerned about being a big somebody. Self-importance in found purely in the love of their caretaker. They have entrusted their lives into their hands and they go about living. If the parent calls, for the most part, they listen. As they mature and learn, they may begin to attend a school, or take lessons from other teachers; all this is designed to enable the child to grow into a mature, educated, well rounded citizen equipped to be an asset to society. The time will come, when the child has matured into an adult and is ready to spread his wings and fly into a life of his own. The lessons, love and care have brought him to this place of independence, and he can now begin to make choices for himself, having been trained in wisdom and understanding. These will be an inner guide along his path. *But his journey is his own.*

A teacher or a caregiver has the job of caring for the needs of the child- *until he is able to care for himself.* A teacher or caregiver also has the job of teaching the child how to care for his own needs, of training him how to function in our society. This is their primary purpose; love and passion for the child's success is what prods them along. They have great vision for the child and they ever have in mind that the day will come when the child will leave the nest and listen to a higher call- *the voice within*. And so we establish the purpose of a caregiver or *"overseer"*.

The Disciples of Christ had yet to learn this child-like spirit. They had an argument that you do not see among children:

"And there was also a strife among them, which of them should be accounted the greatest. And Jesus said to them, 'The kings of the Gentiles exercise lordship over them; and they that exercise authority upon them are called benefactors. (People that provide aid, esp. financial) **But among you it shall not be so:** *but he that is greatest among you let him be as the younger; and he that is chief, as he that serves. For which is greater, he that sits at meat, or he that serves? Is not he that sits at meat? But I am among you as he that serves."* (Luke 22:24-27)

It is very evident that Christ did not want there to be a hierarchy among his people. Luke 3:5 quotes an Old Testament scripture, *"Every valley shall be filled, and every mountain and hill shall be brought low;"* Mountains and valleys are often symbolic of people, and in this we see that the ground is made even. The mountain does not tower over the rest. It is brought down and the ones in the valley are filled up. In the kingdom of God, no one is greater than someone else. No position is more important than another; and so we should not treat some as if they are more important. Yet, so much of religion contradicts this fundamental principal.

Pastors are among the most elevated people in religion. They are usually given a stage- a physical elevation which psychologically gives them a greater bearing over their audience. Many stand behind pulpits. The *pulpit has its origins in paganism and it primarily serves to give a sense of self-importance to the one who stands behind it. The pulpit and stage coupled together give the speaker a feeling of power. Pastors are also typically considered to have a "special anointing" from God, which contradicts the written prophecy of God wherein it states, *"And it shall come to pass afterward, that I will pour out my spirit upon all flesh; and your sons and your daughters shall prophesy, your old men shall dream dreams, your young men shall see visions: And also upon the servants and upon the handmaids in those days will I pour out my spirit,"* (Joel 2:28-29) and Peter declared had been fulfilled. (Acts 2)

The word 'pastors' is only found once in the New Testament. It is not capitalized and it is not given any special ranking. In fact, it's mentioned next to last in this list:

"And he gave some, apostles; and some, prophets; and some, evangelists; and some, pastors and teachers; For the perfecting of the saints, for the work of the ministry, for the edifying of the body of Christ: Till we all come in the unity of the faith, and of the knowledge of the Son of God, unto a perfect man, unto the measure of the stature of the fullness of Christ: That we henceforth be no more children, tossed to and fro, and carried about with every wind of doctrine, by the sleight of men, and cunning craftiness, whereby they lie in wait to deceive; But speaking the truth in love, may grow up into him in all things, which is the head, even Christ:" (Ephesians 4:11-15)

The gifts are to given for a purpose- to help each one grow in Christ, *"Till we all come . . ."* Till- meaning there is a stopping point; Till we come to unity, till we all come to know who the Son of God is and what he came for; Till we all come to Christ- a perfect man, to the measure to the stature of the fullness of Christ- filled with Christ- anointed; *God within.* There comes a time, just like that little child, that we should come to this point and when that time comes, we no longer are in need of apostles, prophets, evangelists, pastors and teachers. But we have come to the fullness of Christ- and we now have God within to be our teacher: *"But the anointing which you have received of him abides in you, and you do not need any man to teach you: but as the same anointing teaches you of all things, and is truth, and is no lie, and even as it has taught you, you shall abide in him."* (1 John 2:27) Just as that little child eventually grows up and is now equipped to live life on his own, so are we to grow up in Christ and the ministry is there to enable us to come to that place where we can be led by the voice of God *within*.

Too many churches misrepresent the place of the ministry, leaving a huge emphasis on all of God's people needing to be under shepherding their entire lives. The *'apostles'* were the original witnesses of Christ Jesus and spreaders of his gospel. *'Prophets'* can help us understand prophecy and even see into the future at times, in order to prepare people for upcoming hardships or needs. *'Evangelists'* are for people who have never heard of the gospel of Jesus Christ. *'Pastors'* and *'teachers'* are to help those that have *heard* the gospel, to *understand* the gospel. They are there to instruct and to guide, in *order to equip people to follow the voice of God within*. None of these offices are more anointed or more important than the other. I even take the stance that later New Testament scriptures have been discolored by people who had become very religious minded, rather than focused on the Word within, and consequently were influenced by hierarchy. A little research into biblical history can support this.

When a church emphasizes the importance of the minister above the rest, when a pastor is held up as a special man of God, able to see more clearly than others, because of a special anointing, a breach is made among God's people; they are crippled in their growth and in their ability to "grow-up to the fullness of Christ."

This fosters a dependency on men rather than a relationship with Christ within.

Consider the body of Christ: *"But speaking the truth in love, may grow up into him in all things, which is the head, even Christ: From whom the whole body fitly joined together and compacted by that which every joint supplies, according to the effectual working in the measure of every part, makes increase of the body unto the edifying of itself in love."* (Ephesians 4:15-16)

A body does not have two heads, unless it is deformed. Most bodies have only one head. There is no "under-head" to help out the chief head. The members do not take instructions from one another. Only one member, the brain, gives instructions. We know that the head is Christ which is the anointing. The hand does not take instructions from the heart, nor do the feet from the legs. Yet they work together, under one head. They each have very different functions:

"For the body is not one member, but many. If the foot shall say, because I am not the hand, I am not of the body; is it therefore not of the body? And if the ear shall say, because I am not the eye, I am not of the body; is it therefore not of the body? If the whole body were an eye, where would the hearing be? If the whole were hearing, where would the smelling be? But now God has set every one of members in the body, as it has pleased him. And if they were all one member, where would the body be? But now are they many members, yet one body. And the eye cannot say to the hand, 'I have no need of you:' nor again the head to the feet, 'I have no need of you.' No, much more those members of the body, which seem to be feebler, are necessary: And those members of the body, which we think to be less honorable, upon these we bestow more abundant honor; and our uncomely parts have more abundant comeliness. For our comely parts have no needs: but God has tempered the body

together, having given more abundant honor to that part which lacked: That there should be no schism in the body; but that the members should have the same care one for another. And if one member suffers, all the members suffer with it; or one member is honored, all the members rejoice with it. Now you are the body of Christ, and members in particular. And God has set some in the gathering; first there are apostles, secondarily prophets, thirdly teachers, after that, miracle workers, then gifts of healings, helps, governments, diversities of tongues. Are all apostles? Are all prophets? Are all teachers? Are all workers of miracles? Have all the gifts of healing? Do all speak with tongues? Do all interpret?" (1 Corinthians 12:14-30)

Here we do not even see "pastors" mentioned. Schism is discord, separation, and disharmony. To set some apart as "special" is to create schism in the body of Christ. Why do so many pastors receive a lofty paycheck and the teachers and other workers do not? Why are pastors considered so much more important in much of today's religious systems than the rest of the body? Why, in so many "fundamentalist churches," are they making rules that the people are told are from God and made to obey? Why??? I have been told it is in order to keep the people "holy and unspotted by the world." Yet, within that very answer lays heresy, for you usurp the authority of Christ and his teaching- that he would give the people a *new heart* and a *new spirit* and by these they would be kept of God. They must lay down their reliance on the spirit of God within, and pick up the Old Testament, Mt. Sinai call to the commandments to avoid the wrath of God. Christ said, *"It shall not be so among you."* (Luke 22:26)

The purpose of any office is for the particular work of seeking the lost, teaching them about Christ- the anointed and the anointing- and to help them learn how to *listen* and to *hear* the voice of God within their *own* soul. It is to reconnect them with

85

God- it is a ministry of *reconciliation*. (2 Corinthians 5:18) Any system that goes beyond this, demanding allegiance to their way of doing things, to their rules, dress codes, and all their do's and don'ts, has usurped Christ's authority.

The main purpose of the pastor was to the *feed the sheep*- feed those who are unable to feed themselves. Also, it is to warn them of danger; to keep them safe from wolves. When those letters were written, most people could not even read. They depended on others to feed them for so long because they were incapable of feeding their selves. And the whole idea of listening within was foreign to them. They had been ruled by religious leaders for hundreds of generations. We are in a different era now.

Christ said that he came among us as a servant. A servant does not get a paycheck. Though they may be cared for by those they serve, they are not a big somebody that has special places or seats in the congregation and everyone goes out of their way to shake their hand like they are a celebrity. When we see this, we are looking upon what Christ called himself- hypocrites. When we allow this we are partaking of the leaven of the Pharisees. **The pastor is not the boss of God's people!** He is to be a man of wisdom that has matured enough in Christ to help support the babes in Christ. The sheep should not feel *intimidated* by him, but rather *loved and cared for*.

There is a great need for Pastors that are truly after God's own heart. I believe most pastors think they are after God's heart but the problem is, they too are conditioned by a religious system that has nothing to do with the message of Jesus Christ. What is the heart-desire of God? Reconciliation with YOU and I! Just as John the Baptist said of Christ, *"He must increase and I must decrease."* He was meaning that Christ, who was the anointed one and came to open the way for us all to be anointed ones, was now all encompassing. John had fulfilled his calling; He had prepared a people ready for the Lord. The people came to John, but now they were ready to look to Christ *alone*. John had no special self-importance that ranked him over others. He simply fulfilled his calling.

The mighty pastor is not mighty at all. *He is a man.* He is flesh and blood like you and I. He is not better than us, more important than us, neither is he to be lifted up, strictly obeyed or to Lord over God's people. His place is not to be a prominent place where we strew his path with palm leaves and cater to his every whim. His place is to serve, to bow his back and his heart to the feet of mankind, and wash away the dirt and toil; He is to refresh and to restore the weary soul. He sits not on a throne, but kneels at an altar and weeps for souls. He is to be so gentle among the people of God, as a nurse cherishes her children she cares for. He is to consider himself whenever he has correction, lest he fall into the same temptation. The calling is a great calling from Christ, because it is a calling of *service* and *sacrifice*.

Like one of my friends told a pastor who wanted her to join their church but first sign a contract that listed a bunch of rules she must adhere to:

"Where is the ointment for my wounds? Where is the cool water for my thirst? When I see you bow at my feet and wash them, when you have poured out oil and bound up my wounds, when you have placed me on your own donkey and taken me to the inn, and paid by the sweat of your own brow for my care, when you have done these things, then I will consider your request. You want me to obey your rules and to become my boss? I do not need any more bosses. I need God's words of comfort; I need friendship, love and care. I already have a boss- the Lord Jesus Christ!"

*The Pulpit and its Origins:

wickedshepherds.com/ThePulpit.html

Chapter 9

If Thine Eye be Single

"It's not what you look at that matters; it's what you see."

-Henry David Thoreau

"The light of the body is the eye. If therefore thine eye be single, thy whole body shall be full of light. But if thine eye be evil, thy whole body shall be full of darkness. If therefore the light that is in thee be darkness, how great is that darkness! "No man can serve two masters; for either he will hate the one and love the other, or else he will hold to the one and despise the other. Ye cannot serve God and mammon." (Matthew 6: 22-24)

Many newer translations of this scripture have translated the phrase, *"If thine eye be single"* so many different ways; *"if thine eye be simple, if thine eye be sincere, if thine eye can be perfect, if thine eye be healthy. . ."* But the original King James and the 21st Century King James translate this as "single". A deeper look into the meaning behind the "single" eye can shed some light on what Jesus may have been trying to convey here.

In eastern religion, as far back as history has been recorded, they have taught about the "third eye." The *third eye is considered the second sight and, unlike the two eyes we see the world through, it is *single*. This eye is said to be the *pineal gland in the brain and is concentrated between and directly above the eyebrows. Typically, people who have visions that no one else can see, such as Peter seeing the sheet of meat come down out of heaven, is seeing this with their third eye; It is considered the eye of intuition, or the eye that sees beyond the physical world. It is the eye that beholds the light of God within. So with our two physical eyes, we see out into the physical world, but with the inner, *single eye* we see the non-physical world. We are all born with a third eye, but most of us never develop that eye and even close it entirely, due to the outward focus that is emphasized in this world. But even a blind man can see with his third eye if he sets his heart on God.

Now, let's take a look at this scripture in light of the single eye, meaning, looking *within*, rather than looking *without*:

The light of the body is the eye. If therefore the eye you are viewing through is your single eye- the eye that looks within- your whole body is going to be FULL of light. But if your eye is evil- if you are looking through the eyes that see outward, that are focused on all the worlds riches, "the lust of the eyes" (1 John 2:16) then your whole body will be full of darkness. If therefore the light that is in you, comes from your outward perception, how great is that darkness. No man can serve two masters; you can't serve the eye of intuition which is focused upon God within, and the two eyes that are without, that are focused upon the world.

Now, considering the "single" eye as being the eye within, focused on the spiritual, let us consider who or what we are truly serving.

"Not that we are sufficient of ourselves to think of anything as coming from ourselves, but our sufficiency is from God, who also has made us able ministers of the new testament — not of the letter, but of the Spirit; for the letter kills, but the Spirit gives life." (2 Corinthians 3:5-6)

I grew up listening to people of different beliefs passionately fighting over *their interpretation of the letter* being the truth. I witnessed heated, red-faced arguments with clenched fists, and disgust spewed from lips, all in a quest to defend "their God" and "his truth." In my adulthood, I too fell into this miry digression, believing God was well pleased with my courage to "face the foe and stand for truth." All the while the little four-letter word, **L-O-V-E**, that God identifies as *himself*, was stuffed into a self-righteous corner and I joined the corporate banter that even Jesus used a whip and upturned tables in his fury, to justified my position. Meanwhile, relationships turned sour, and I went on, blinded to the chains that were steadily forged year by year around my entire world. I had a master alright- the master of my own two physical eyes- the master of the letter of the law. It would be 18 years before I was set free, and once again, let the eye of the body be single.

That pivotal point came one morning, while reading from Hebrews 12:

"For ye have not come unto the mount which might be touched and that burned with fire, nor unto blackness and darkness and tempest, and the sound of a trumpet and the voice of words, which voice those who heard entreated that the Word should not be spoken to them anymore. (For they could not endure that which was commanded, that: "if even so much as a beast touch the mountain, it shall be stoned or thrust through with a dart." And so terrible was the sight that Moses said, "I fear exceedingly and quake." (Hebrews 12:18-21)

Though I had read this passage many times before and knew it by heart, I slowed down and reread it over and again, this time *amazed* as I realized that this was *exactly* how I felt. ***I had an Old Testament experience.*** Over the course of the past 18 years, I had been deduced to the keeping of rules, which other men termed as, "the holy standard of God." I had listened faithfully, at a minimum of four times per week, to *"the sound of a trumpet and the voice of words,"* which continually kept me terrified of God.

I continued on reading in Hebrews 12, now in illuminated awe by the light of God within;

"But you have come unto Mount Zion, and to the city of the living God, the heavenly Jerusalem, and to an innumerable company of angels, to the general assembly and church of the firstborn, who are written in Heaven, and to God the Judge of all, and to the spirits of just men made perfect, and to Jesus the Mediator of the new covenant, and to the blood of sprinkling, that speaks of better things than that of Abel. See that you do not refuse Him that speaks from heaven, for if they who refused him that spoke on earth, did not escape, much more shall we not escape if we turn away from Him that speaks from Heaven," (Hebrews 12:22-25)

This was speaking of a *living* God, not a terrible, beastly God of death written down on paper and passed down through generations. Also, the church I had been attending taught that to *"refuse him that speaks from heaven"* meant to refuse the message the pastor brought; for the pastor went and received his message from heaven. But Spirit within me was showing me clearly how this scripture states, that the *man* is the one who speaks on earth. **The voice from heaven is his loving, calming, living presence within. This was about the "Word" within.** It was about listening to, and hearing Spirit's voice above all others and not refusing what that voice from heaven is speaking because of what the two physical eyes that look without have come to see and understand.

God was challenging me, to lay down my religious cloak, to let go of all that I had heretofore learned, and to listen solely to him. Like Saul of old, I was arrested that morning, and shown that all that I had hitherto gained in religion was but dung in comparison to the constant Holy Communion he had prepared, within my own heart.

Religion stills the voice of God within. Religion places our focus on pastors and teachers, on programs, creeds and disciplines, and on trying to figure out the right interpretation of scriptures. It conveys to you the message that only certain people that are specially chosen of God can truly hear his voice and the rest of us must pay attention and obey what is coming from without. But as we have established in previous chapters, Christ was the fulfillment of the promise that everyone could have the spirit of God poured out on them. (Acts 1)

"Search the scriptures; for in them you think you have eternal life: and theses are they which testify of me." (John 5:39)

You can study and interpret the scripture (letter) until the cows come home, but that is not where abundant life is; abundant life is within the spirit. *Scripture does not define nor dictate the Word, but rather, the Word, when living within our hearts, defines and dictates the scripture.* The Word is God; God is I Am; I AM a child of God; I AM saved; I AM holy; I AM pure in heart; I AM because of the Word *within* me. I AM free- free to be God's child alone. I AM free to listen and to hear the Word *within me.*

If I turn from the Word within that speaks from heaven and begin to make the scripture (letter) into my God, I will die, because "the letter kills." It's dead food. It is not the bread of life nor the water that quenches your thirst. *Christ- I AM- the Word within, is the bread of life and the cool clear water.* Christ provides FRESH manna from heaven every day, manna that is suitable, tailor picked, for our very personal and intimate needs in life. Sometimes he will use the Bible in his conversation with us. The Bible is a blessing and a gift. But spirits voice within is what we must come to intimately know.

To illustrate the difference more clearly, we read in 1 Timothy 2:9-10 *"In like manner also, that women should adorn themselves in modest apparel, with shamefacedness and a sober mind, not with braided hair or gold or pearls or costly array, but, as that which is becoming to women professing godliness, with good works."*

I can read this scripture and learn from it; *but it is not a commandment* written in stone by the finger of God that if I do not perfectly obey, I will be condemned, or God will now be angry with me. It is a *letter*, written by a *person* that was doing their best to hear God, who felt moved to address a particular need peculiar to that congregation, culture and time. Through this scripture, I am able to draw a principle worth adding to the building blocks of my life; I pray, I read and I am enlightened that the principal was one of modesty and not placing my focus on outward beauty and attraction, but rather to be more concerned about the hidden person- *the life within*, the spirit. But I am still FREE- free to wear a wedding ring or a necklace or earrings. I still have FREEDOM the Word, within my own heart and soul *my* master. My eye is single. If I should hear Spirit speak to me as I am putting on a particular piece of jewelry, and say, *"Liz, do not wear that,"* I will listen and obey - not out of fear- but because I have come to love and trust in this inner friend so much; This voice within has become my truest ally- my guide that never fails. This Word within is a precious treasure and I rejoice when it speaks to me, for I know it leads me to still waters and green pastures. It is my inner guide, seen, not with my outer eyes, but with my *single* eye.

But just because God tells me to not wear that necklace, does not mean it is now my responsibility to inform everyone that serves God that necklaces are evil. *God will always have different instructions for different people.* I challenge you to show me two identical biblical stories in which God gave the exact same instructions. It will not be found. Because every person, each situation, is *unique*. So I can entrust your soul into God's hands. I can share what I am learning; I can write about it, as I am now doing. But I have to leave what God shows you, with you. Even what people take away from this book will greatly vary. Some people might love it, while others may hate and condemn it. I have to leave it with them to decide.

Let us not therefore judge one another any longer. But rather judge this; that no man put an offense before another or an occasion to fall in his brother's way. I know and am convinced in the Lord Jesus that **there is nothing unholy of itself: But to him that thinks it is unholy, to him it is unholy.** (Romans 14)

Religion builds their walls on the letter; thus we have multitudes of interpretations, for no two people can ever have the exact same perception. Each division judges the next by their personal convictions. They become like the blind men in the parable that are all feeling a giant elephant from different sides, and arguing about what it looks like.

I go to such lengths in this, because the world of Christianity is becoming a farce to outsiders. Why? Division, and the ugly fighting, shunning, wall building and much worse that has been done in the name of Jesus! Too many that call themselves Christians, have closed up their single eye within, and see only with their outer eyes; so many have ceased to hear the voice of God within. *"Therefore I speak to them in parables: because they seeing see not; and hearing they hear not, neither do they understand."* (Matthew 13:13)

It's not that we need to agree on everything; we need to come to a place that we recognize and respect each one as individuals on their own journey, and that no two people can ever have the exact same perception. We need to encourage one another to listen to the voice of God within. In the religious world there is so much division and contention. But the voice of God within, being heeded, and respected in one another, will lead us to harmony.

"I have given them your word; and the world has hated them, because they are not of the world, even as I am not of the world. I pray not that you should take them out of the world, but that you should keep them from the evil. They are not of the world, even as I am not of the world. Sanctify them through your truth: you word is truth. As you have sent me into the world, even so have I also sent them into the world. And for their sakes I sanctify myself, that they also might be sanctified through the truth. Neither pray I for these alone, but for them also which shall believe on me through their word; That they all may be one; as you, Father, are in me, and I am in you, that they also may be one in us: that the world may believe that you have sent me. And the glory which you gave me I have given them; that they may be one, even as we are one: I in them, and you in me, that they may be made perfect in one; and that the world may know that you have sent me, and have loved them, as you have loved me. (John 17: 14-23)

There is so much more I could say here. Jesus said that whatever you do to the least of humankind- you do to him. He was teaching oneness; what we do to one, we do to all. (Matthew 25:40)

So the question is, *is your eye single?*

ThirdEyePinecones.com/history-symbolism

Mysticbanana.com/pineal-gland-our-third-eye-the-biggest-cover-up-in-human-history.html

Chapter 10

Imprinting

"Generally by the time you are real, most of your hair has been loved off, and your eyes drop out and you get loose in your joints and very shabby. But these things don't matter at all because once you are real you can't be ugly... except to people who don't understand."

- The Velveteen Rabbit

In nature, it is said that a newborn animal will believe that whoever it first comes into contact with, and cares for it, that is its mother; it is termed, *imprinting*. In a very real sense, we as humans are imprinted as well. Each one of us entered into this world helpless and poor. We were surrounded by unique people in various cultures. We were each raised within differing beliefs, customs, values and personalities. Even those born on the same day, in the same hospital, with the same cultural background will differ greatly. Some will have loving, nurturing parents; others will have to struggle through life in a very unhealthy and unloving environment. Some will have homes where faith is strong and traditions are important. Others will never be taught about God at all. Some will be born strong and healthy; others will be sickly, mentally handicapped or crippled.

And so, we all entered our lives here on earth, in incalculable sorts of environments and circumstances and these environments and circumstances *imprint* us. We grow up, and just like the animal in the wild, we believe all our own senses; they are what is real to us, whether or not anyone else believes it. Each one of us has our own unique and personal experience of life. No two perceptions can ever be exactly the same.

In Romans 14, the Bible teaches us that nothing in and of itself is unclean. But to those that think something is unclean-according to their unique understanding and perception- to them it is unclean. And so the Bible says that we should not be judging one another, because we are all so unique, and if something is wrong to you, it may not be wrong to the next person. But for you, if it is wrong to you, and you go ahead and partake of it anyway, just because someone else does, you will defile your conscience. You will feel like Adam and Eve did when they partook of the forbidden fruit. You will feel a need to hide from God, instead of being free in his presence.

Conversely, if you believe something is okay, perhaps you feel free to drink a little wine and are not tempted to drunkenness. But you know your friend is so against even sipping on wine. Then, when you are in the company of your friend, you ought to forfeit the wine for that time and respect your friends conscience, that you do not tempt him to override what he believes is wrong.

Imprinting affects every one of us whether we like it or not. But if you would grow up in God, you need to allow the voice of God within to challenge your preconceived ideas of what truth is. When you allow this, God will rock your world. You will experience a spiritual earthquake, I guarantee it! The spiritual earthquake will remove from your spiritual life, that which is not solid. (Hebrews 12:27) Spiritual earthquakes will open prison doors; (Matthew 28:2, Acts 16:26) Spiritual earthquakes will fill you with the Spirit of God; (Acts 4:31) It is essential to our spiritual growth that we seek God with all our heart, soul, mind and strength and we allow *Spirit* to teach us.

It has been said, "Question everything." One of the most liberating revelations I ever received from God is that God is not threatened by our questions, no matter what they are. Who of us, as parents, chastise our children because they question us? If we do, we will stunt their growth. Questions are vital to their understanding of the world. Educational systems stake so much value in questions that they spend immense amount of time teaching pupils *how* to question- how to look at things from every angle through questioning. Technology would never advance without questions. If I were to question even the very existence of God, that is still no threat to God. It makes him no less God; however, it does open wide a door for God to be able to answer my questions in so many ways, and manifest to truth to me. You may immediately think of the scripture that states, *"The fool has said in his heart, there is no God."* (Psalms 14:1) However, this is not a question. It is a resolute statement- a very important difference.

"Why?" This is a very telling little question. Try asking why about a typical religious belief and continue asking why until you can no longer answer. What do notice that goes on *inside* of you?

The following are a simple question with their typical answers I have been told over the years.

Why are we here?

God created us.

Why did God create us?

He was lonely and wanted to have souls made in his image.

Why did he want us made in his image?

He already had angels that worshipped him but only did so by instinct. He wanted men to choose to worship him from their own free will.

Why did he want men to choose to worship him?

Hmmm...Good question!

Let's do another one:

Why did God create hell?

To put those who do not love him supremely in.

Why does God want everyone to love him supremely?

Hmmm...Good question!

Why would God put people in a place to be tormented forever?

They would not accept his sacrifice of his son to take away their sins.

Why does he want to take away our sins?

Because he loves you and wants you to be with him, but he is so holy that he cannot stand to be in the presence of a sinner.

Why is he so holy?

Hmmm...Good question!

What becomes so interesting when you do this is you begin to see how ludicrous some beliefs really are- how they don't really add up or make any sense. When you start to really think about the answers that you might put in place of the "good question" you realize that we are describing a God who has been portrayed throughout time as very arrogant and egotistical.

"When Jesus came into the region of Caesarea Philippi, He asked His disciples, saying, "Who do men say that I, the Son of man, am?" And they said, "Some say that you are John the Baptist, some say Elijah, and others Jeremiah or one of the prophets." He said to them, But

whom do you say that I am? And Simon Peter answered and said, "You are the Christ, the Son of the living God." And Jesus answered and said to him, "You are blessed, Simon Bar-Jonah, for flesh and blood has not revealed this to you, but My Father who is in Heaven." (Matthew 16: 13-17)

"Then He charged His disciples that they should tell no man that He was Jesus the Christ. From that time forth Jesus began to share with His disciples that He must go to Jerusalem and suffer many things of the elders and chief priests and scribes, and be killed, and be raised again the third day. Then Peter took Him and began to rebuke Him, saying, "Be it far from you, Lord; this shall not happen to you." But He turned and said to Peter, "You get behind Me, Satan! You are an offense to me; for you do not savor the things that are of God, but those that are of men." (Matthew 16: 20-23)

Two important lessons happened to Peter within a short amount of time. In the first, Peter heard the voice of God within. God had revealed to Peter that Jesus was indeed the Christ- the anointed one. And Jesus knew by Peter's direct affirmation of his deity, that only God could have revealed this to him. He told Peter that he was blessed to have been given this revelation. But then, a little later, we see this same Peter passionately rebuking Christ and what he was revealing to them. You see, this time, Peter was leaning on his own *spiritual imprinting* from what he had been taught about the Christ. He understood that Christ was to be King, not hang like some common criminal on a cross. The disciples were excited to be a part of this great ushering in of a new millennium, where this Jesus would sit on David's throne and they would be his loyal and honorable subjects. But to be associated with a criminal condemned to death- *"Not so Lord! This shall not happen to you!"* At that moment in time, as with other future moments in time, Peter would struggle between what *he understood* about the Kingdom of God, and what was really the truth about the kingdom

101

of God. Later we read about the struggle over allowing Gentiles into the church, and doing away with circumcision and the old Hebrew law. In all these things, the people of God would need to learn how to discern the voice of God within.

And so it's been throughout Christian history. Spiritual movements are not usually preceded by a message preached from a pulpit, but by a personal revelation- an anointing from the holy spirit of God. But, due to our original imprinting that we all have, many of us never remove ourselves far enough away from it and question the validity of our beliefs. We do not examine them from every angle and allow Spirit to teach us *something new*. Most people just adopt some sort of belief system and then just sort of become a stick in the mud with it. And they end up earthbound, grasping into thin air for the things of the spirit such as joy, peace, gentleness, goodness, faith. Feeling frustrated, many become complacent and/or fear to ruffle the waters.

Just like the impotent man who laid year after year by the waters of Bethesda, for the angel to come and stir the waters; For he knew that if he was the first to get into the waters after they were stirred, he would be instantly healed. It took a messenger from heaven to stir up the waters and a very eager and willing soul to jump in and be healed. But the impotent man lay in his bed of excuses, waiting for men of flesh and blood to come and serve his need; for, due to his infirmity, he could never make it into the waters before someone else stepped in ahead of him and claimed their healing. This is allegorical of the many that wait on the preacher, the pastor, the church system to come to their rescue and lift them out of their crippling condition. But one day, Christ came by and challenged this man's entire paradigm. He let the man know he did not even need the waters- he told him, *"Rise up, pick up your bed and walk."* Jesus conveyed the message to this man that they only thing that stood between him and his healing was his *beliefs-*

his mindset. This man had been *imprinted* with the idea that his only hope was this pool of water stirred by the angel. But Christ taught him that the power of the kingdom of God was *within* him. (John 5: 2-9)

[?]

Exercise:

1. Write down your top ten beliefs. You can add more later, but for now, write no less than ten. (E.g. 1. God created everything, 2. There is a heaven that good people go to, 3. Jesus is the only way to heaven, ...)

2. Next, for each belief answer these next questions
   a) Where did this belief come from?
   b) When did you first learn this belief?
   c) Who or what else has reinforced this belief?
   d) What is the purpose of this belief?
   e) How does this belief positively affect your life?
   f) How does this belief negatively affect your life?

Write out your questions and answers. Take your time; work a little every day on it if you need to. Notice any patterns in your answers. If negative emotions arise, acknowledge them and sit with them for a while. Let your emotions and patterns teach you. Listen to what the voice of God within is saying about these beliefs.

This is a very powerful exercise and the more strong beliefs you add the more you will benefit from it. Remember, beliefs are just that- they are believed. We do not normally question our beliefs, or if we do have questions, we often pass it off as doubt and not worthy of our attention. But beliefs shape and define us and it is worth knowing that we can confidently answer these questions about them.

Chapter 11

Spirit and Truth

"God is a Spirit, and they that worship Him must worship Him in spirit and in truth." (John 4:24)

I personally believe that this scripture is one of the most misunderstood teachings of Christ, and is responsible for so much division. The deeply held conviction of most of Christianity is that "spirit and truth" are the baptizing of the holy spirit and the one truth that everyone keeps looking for- that one infallible teaching that we must figure out and then diligently follow lest we fall into eternal destruction. But I would like to challenge this, for I have had a personal revelation about this scripture. First, let's place it in the context in which it was written.

Jesus was passing through Samaria. The Samaritans were people that the Jews held in disdain. The Bible says the Jews did not even deal with them at all. And so this Samaritan woman was taken aback when Jesus spoke to her:

"The woman of Samaria said to Him, 'How is it that you, being a Jew, ask me for a drink, who is a woman of Samaria?' For the Jews have no dealings with the Samaritans. Jesus answered her and said, 'If you understood the gift of God and who it is that said to you, 'Give Me a drink,' you would have asked of Him, and He would have given you living water.' The woman said to Him, 'Sir, you have nothing to draw with, and the well is deep. From where then do you have that living water? Are you greater than our father Jacob, who gave us this well and drank out of it himself, as well as his children and his cattle?' Jesus answered and said to her, 'Who ever drinks of the water from this well, shall thirst again; but whoever drinks of the water that I shall give him shall never thirst; but the water that I

*shall give him **shall be in him** a well of water springing up into everlasting life.' The woman said to Him, 'Sir, give me this water, that I thirst not, neither come hither to draw.' Jesus said to her, 'Go, call thy husband, and come hither.' The woman answered and said, 'I have no husband.' Jesus said to her, 'you have well said, 'I have no husband'; for you have had five husbands, and the one you now have is not your husband. In this you have spoken truly.' The woman said to Him, 'Sir, I perceive that you are a prophet. Our fathers worshiped on this mountain, and you say that Jerusalem is the place where men ought to worship.' Jesus said to her, 'Woman, believe me, the hour comes when you shall neither on this mountain, nor yet at Jerusalem, worship the Father. You do not know what you worship; we know what we worship, for salvation is of the Jews. But the hour comes and is now, when the true worshipers shall worship the Father in spirit and in truth; for the Father seeks such to worship Him. God is a Spirit, and they that worship Him must worship Him in spirit and in truth."* (John 4: 7-24)

I would like to contend that the spirit and *truth here are *"within your spirit and in a true character."* This truth he is speaking about is not an infallible doctrine, but rather a true and honest character- someone who is willing to listen to Spirit's voice within and to follow. The woman tried to pull out the age-old argument over where the true worshippers were to worship. But she was pointing to things *without-* places, people, and teachings. Christ pulled her back and said essentially, *God is not interested in this argument. What he desires are worshippers that will worship him within their spirit, and with a true and honest character.* When we allow the true meaning to shine through the Bible, prison doors are unlocked and the captives are truly set free. We realize that dogma has been a dictator, and is not what Christ demonstrated nor taught. In fact, he demonstrated quite the opposite.

One of my earliest childhood memories was when I was around 2-3 years old. I wandered alone in the backyard, mesmerized by all the beauty and awe about me. I peeled off golden snails glued to our stucco house and gently touched their little antennas watching them disappear and then reappear again. The spiraling pattern on the fragile shell, and their sticky body fascinated me. Daddy-long-legs tickled my arms and roly-polies would not stay open no matter how much I coaxed. This was a preverbal time of my life, and I did not have the words I now have to describe all that seduced me in the backyard morning sunlight. At a certain level, I identified with the shy little creatures that but a waif of wind sent them hiding into their shells; for at the tender age of two, my heart already understood how dangerous and unpredictable life could be. But quiet moments such as these possessed me with wonder and awe.

Suddenly I became mysteriously drawn to this big, full bloomed, crimson-red rose covered with tiny dew drops glistening in the light of the sun. I was riveted by its enchanting beauty. This magical moment of God's glory revealing itself in creation and my inward worship of it all, has stayed with me throughout my life. I was innately aware of God's presence then. He had not yet been given the name "God" or "Spirit" or anything else. There was no form introduced to my innocent mind. I had not yet been drummed with lessons about who *he* was, nor what his expectations of me were. I was simply, and purely aware of the presence in me, and all around me. I was conscious that I and everything my eyes were beholding was part of the essence of I AM. And from the inner springs of that innocent little child, *I was worshipping in the purest sense*. I understood that I was a precious treasure placed here for a purpose. *"The King is held in the galleries."* (Song 7:5) Yet, through the hardships and trauma I was to pass through, I would quickly lose, for many years, that sense of God's pure love and light.

Life is a battle from conception. Cradled in a warm womb, danger lurks from all the powers that be, that would destroy us or traumatize us, even hidden in the watery baptismal. Suddenly we are birthed, violently pushed out of the warm and dark resting place, into bright lights, noise, and distraction everywhere. We struggle to find that first gust of air that will be called upon continuously to keep us alive. Our voice is discovered in an unintentional wail for relief of the first sense of pain and insecurity, for we have no idea how to communicate our discomfort, fear or needs. Some enter with ferocious battles for life, while others are more comparatively mild. But one thing is absolutely, unequivocally true for us all, we enter with a certain power- God *within*! Before we are born, before anyone ever has a chance to define God by name, beliefs and expectations, *we already innately know him*. He is our breath- the very breath of life. He is the grandeur of the Sun and the melodious song of nature. He is in everything and everything is of Him!

"In the beginning was the Word, and the Word was with God, and the Word was God. The same was in the beginning with God. All things were made by Him, and without Him was not anything made that was made. In Him was life, and that life was the Light of men." (John 1:1-4)

God is not a "him"- it is just the only way my English knows how to give reference; nor is God a "she." God is not flesh and blood like we are here in this physical dimension. *God is spirit*. And true worship is in spirit and truth (honesty). The title 'God' is a universal language to know how to give substance to the all-powerful, all-encompassing spirit - through whom *"we live, and move, and have our being;"* (Acts 17:28)

We have come into this world to learn and to grow and to understand Spirit in a more intimate way. But in order for this to happen, we must be challenged by the *opposite* of Spirit. You cannot know light without experiencing darkness. You cannot know love without understanding hate. In order to know what something *is*, you have to understand what it is *not*. We know that God is Love. The opposite of love is hate. Spirit is peace; the opposite of peace is war; Spirit is life- the opposite of life is death. And Spirit is all powerful- the opposite of power is vulnerability, or *disempowerment*.

Spirit knows what will make us strong, healthy, peaceful, joyful, and full of love. Spirit is within- a guiding force that enable us to defeat every demon that would disempower us. So darkness reaches its icy frigid fingers out to disempower every human that comes into this time world, and the quickest, most efficient way to do this is to **silence** Spirit within. And so from the time of conception, we are accosted from *without* to draw us away from Spirit within, and so surrender our personal power to the powers that be without. The dark powers of this world seek to take up the residence within, that rightly belongs to Spirit and to bring us into bondage and slavery. This is why so many of us grow up into this world feeling like victims of circumstance, rather than a co-creator of our destiny and a powerful entity or expression of Spirit.

Because God is love, Spirit loves us so completely, so purely and it is ever in Spirits heart to turn us back within and set us free once more. But Spirit is all wise as well, and knows that true consecration can only come from one that comes to recognize the pure and beautiful, priceless love Spirit has for them. This is why Christ was manifest into this world. Christ Jesus' entire purpose was to realign us back with Spirit. But some people have been so victimized under the name of God that this seems impossible, unless they can relearn God as Spirit, or as inner guide, and forget all they were taught of God and begin to *listen to the voice of God within.*

Jesus' death was for us- it was a gift to set us free from the bondage of the powers of this world. It was to give us back our power in Spirit. Somewhere along life's journey, people became convinced that all their wrongs had to be righted by blood shed- and the sacrificing of animals ensued. This became an ingrained belief and the only way this could be overcome, was for Christ to be able to say, *"Look, I lived a perfect life. I had no cause to be punished. And so I am going to shed my blood for you, so you can now have my righteous life within you and the blood I shed will take care of all you believe you have done wrong. Turn away from the sins that defile your conscience. I will teach you all about what the real love of God truly is. I came to give you a NEW heart and a NEW spirit and to show you the way of LOVE- for greater love has no man than he who lays down his life for his friends. Yet I take love even further- I lay down my life for those who are yet separated from me, because of being disempowered and brought into bondage by the dark powers of this world, by spiritual wickedness in high places. I make a way through my sacrificial love for all to unite in spirit and truth- in SPIRIT- in GOD- in LOVE and in a true and honest character! I came to set the captives free, to open the prison doors, to heal the broken in heart and bind up their wounds. I came in SPIRIT and in TRUTH!*

(See "truth" @ Dictionary.com/browse/truth)

Exercises:

B) Slow down; take time to notice the glory of God all around you, in the little things. Write or draw as you see them. Take note of the natural worship that arises within your spirit. "STOP and smell the roses!" Bend down and pet the cat, watch the sunrise, notice the birds flying against the billowy blue sky. Take time to see the stars. Be in awe. Let the wonder of life fill you with the spirit that animates it all.

?

Chapter 12

Religion Verses Reality

"I don't feel obliged to believe that the same God who has endowed us with sense, reason and intellect, has intended us to forego their use."

-Galileo Galilei

It's always those little sentiments- tiny bits of wisdom that come out of the most obscure places that stick and are used to shape our lives. Such was this little thought from a man shattered by unthinkable abuse. I was reaching out to him with "the gospel of Jesus Christ," hoping to give him some sort of solace for all that he had suffered. His response to me was so simplistic and yet extremely profound. Here I was trying to tell him about a heaven beyond this world of confusion and heartache; but he had already settled the question of life. He hadn't denied it, nor had he acknowledged it. He simply responded with the most honest words I had ever been answered- ***"Life is a mystery, and I'm okay with that."***

Of all the horror stories I had ever been confronted with, none compared to the nightmare this man had been born into. Abuse beyond human description was his lot for most of his childhood. He had spent his adulthood trying to heal from the trauma and the havoc it had mentally and emotionally wreaked in his life. But his anchor was not in Jesus, or God, or Buddha; it was not in a philosophy of some sort. His anchor was in *reality*- what *is*- the *present* moment. He had grasped the substance behind, "it is what it is."

Today the call to "be present" is being resounded out everywhere. It is a uniting goal of just about any belief system. To be present is being touted as the way to really be alive and to enjoy life. But I think many times when a teaching becomes very common-place, the real value of it is often lost. And I believe that the point of being in the present moment is the pivotal point of religion verses reality.

Religion, for the most part is grounded in faith, and most of the time it is *blind* faith. There is a difference between blind-faith and faith that is established in evidence. Many people begin listening to Spirit within, and the evidence of that voice within is seen in the workings of their life- they see how that little voice within is faithful to guide them aright. This is a reality. We cannot deny the chatter in our head. And when we begin to ask to discern Spirit's voice above all the others, this voice beings to stand out over the rest. The voice is our own, for we cannot separate it from spirit within. And faith grows in the evidence of this working for us. Too many exchange this evidence-based faith for religion. They do not even realize this is happening for it is subtle, but they exchange faith in the WORD of God- the voice of God within- their REALITY, their TRUTH, for religious beliefs.

Blind faith is anchored in the imagination. Consequently we have innumerable different religious sects; as far and as varied as the imagination can go, which is pretty endless, that is as far and as varied as religious beliefs can go. Religion for the most part is imaginative; it is not based in reality. It's based on the words and beliefs of past generations and cultures that have been imposed upon us. Religion is not based and grounded in our current reality. The only reality we have to deal with is what is right here, right now- the *present*. The past was a reality at one time. But the past reality becomes distorted the further back it gets from this present moment. And the future can ever only be imagination; it is not reality. **To be present is to be grounded in reality.**

Religion doesn't teach you to be grounded in reality. They think they do, by virtue of what they are *not* teaching – i.e. witch-craft or following fables, etc.… They believe they are teaching life as it is. But when you start telling people that they have to believe and follow something that men wrote hundreds, thousands and even millions of years ago within their culture and society- that they have to follow these ancient teachings in order to be a part of their society, or in order to be right in life or with God, then it has ceased to be based in reality. For as we have already established, reality is what is real at this present moment. And so that is what "being present" is about; it's about being grounded in reality- being grounded and focused on what is.

Again, when Moses asked God, who are you? Who should I tell men that you are? God answered, "I am, that I am." Basically he said, "I am! I do not need a label; I do not need to be put in a box. This is just who I am and this is where we are." It didn't have to be explained any further than that.

God is a Spirit and that Spirit is the life force energy of all that it is. You cannot separate God and Spirit nor can you separate anything in our reality from Spirit. If in God "we live and move and exist" then you cannot ever be separate from God (Acts 17:28).

Belief systems help people to make sense of this life; and church is a place where people gather with other people of like beliefs to have those beliefs validated and to feel a sense of safety and purpose.

When I asked God years ago to please "take the religious spirit out of me," I had no idea that he would ultimately dissolve the religious filters I was viewing life through and completely break down my entire idea of who God was. Indeed it was very scary. For to break down the religious beliefs of an individual, is to break down their connection with the community they belong to, to take away the crutches of validation and to toss that person out into the universal sea to sink or swim. It is to rip the rug from underneath them so they can get their roots down into the earth- or reality.

Religion had given me a sense of belonging, a sense of purpose and a sense of safety. I was safe from the snares of sin, the dangers in this world, safe from eternal torture and even safe from myself. Religion allowed me to hide from fear as it took the responsibility of my life out of my hands and placed it on the system's idea of God. But it cost me my individuality, my freedom of choice, my own discernment, and the governing of my home and family. I had to answer to an easily angered God (at least that is how I perceived him by how he was preached) for everything I did, robbing me of my trust in God's love for me, and it stunted my growth- for growth can only come by making mistakes with an understanding that mistakes are necessary and okay. When you tell a child he better keep his room clean or he is going to get a beating, you have done nothing to teach him responsibility or the value of a clean room. You have taught him *fear* and *dread* and that something must be done in order to appease the aggressor, not for the sake of the rightness of doing it.

Religion cannot be based in reality as long as it requires an individual to hold to a systems ways over their own internal voice of God. For the only true reality a person has is the present moment. What God told the Virgin Mary, is going to be completely different to what he tells 14 year old Jane Doe, impregnated by her abuser in the 21st century.

Religion cannot be based in reality when it does not allow you to be *real.* It cannot be reality when you have to deny yourself, your inner voice, your intuition, and your truth, in order to live out its mandates. Being present and being still and listening within, trusting your intuition, listening to your needs and taking care of yourself, listening to your truth and honoring it, these are all grounded in reality. They will bring you strength, peace, trust and light. To *"love God with all your heart soul mind and strength"* is to honor the voice within; to *"love your neighbor as yourself"* is to love the voice within; to *"judge not, that you be not judged"* is to validate the voice within others.

When Jesus told the religious leaders of his day, "You are of your father the devil," they were looking at God as a fatherly figure, and they were telling Jesus that he couldn't possibly be a part of God because he was teaching and doing things outside their box of religious conduct. And so he brought the thought of the devil as a father as well. And basically the connotation to them was that they had dark works- they were of darkness. Jesus never came to teach us about a heaven and a hell and a duality. He came to teach us oneness. He came to set us free from duality. And he came to show us that the way to be free from duality is to walk in the light of the Word- the truth that you have *within* you.

Jesus taught that God seeks those that worship in spirit and truth. Worship is a very nebulous word. It is like the word love; there is no way you can completely define love. Ask several people to define love. Some may say it's bringing someone flowers and having a wine and candlelight dinner. Or some might say its having strong feeling of care and concern for somebody. You try to define love and it is difficult- difficult to put a definition on it; because love encompasses so much. And it is the same with worship.

Worship in Spirit is in knowing that God is Spirit and that everything in reality has its basis and its life force from this Spirit. And so when you look within to that life force, which is God, and are able to come to that place of awe for life- that place of complete passion and inspiration- that *awe* encompasses worship. Worship will manifest in different ways, just like love may be manifested in someone bringing you flowers or someone holding you or perhaps doing something to help you. It's the same thing with worship. Worship is going to manifest itself in a variety of ways in different people. It may manifest in somebody setting up a little altar and thinking about God, and just being in awe of God, the Spirit and of life; maybe in another person it will come out in doing good to other people because they are just so awe-inspired by this good and sovereign spirit that is within all. And so worship is a very all-encompassing word. And when we are allowing ourselves to worship from within and according to the truth we have within our hearts, we are worshipping in spirit and truth and it is based in reality rather than religion. True worship is not a public demonstration to conformity of a religion's ideology. It is something that flows naturally from within.

Sometimes we need to just whittle away the nonsensical debris of life and just come back to the core. And the core of life is reality- it is presence. The only thing that we know undoubtedly in this world is our presence- like God said, "I am that I am." I know I am a woman on earth, in America, in California, having an experience of life here. These are realities that I do not need to have a blind faith in. They are obvious. When you whittle life down to, *I am here, and I am experiencing and I am learning as I go- that is what I know-* that is reality. Beyond that, everything else is speculation. Everything else is how you are trying to make sense out of life. Every religion, every thought, every belief is speculation.

When the Apostle Paul was telling the king that he wanted him to know the truth, the king replied, "What is truth?" Truth is what Christ teaches; it is oneness; we are really not separate. We are in the same world together and there is a spirit in all of us that is animating each one of us. We each have a life in which we have consciousness and through which we are experiencing our life through individual and unique perceptions. So, **all that we really have is presence and consciousness.** When you whittle it all down to this, it really sets you free; "You will know the truth and the truth will set you free." Suddenly you don't have to know everything or be something or perform somehow. You are now free just to BE! You are learning, growing and expanding - you are conscious and you are experiencing. And beyond that, everything else is a belief based on experiences. When someone takes the belief they formed from their unique life experience and they build a religious practice around it and invite others to come and practice the same thing, based on what they have learned, it becomes a religion. This is okay- until the practice supersedes the voice of God within, or until their practice is taught as superior to others. We should not invalidate another perspective. Because at that point people begin to value some souls more than others and pretty soon atrocities are being committed all in the name of that has religion that left off the voice of God within and embraced blind faith.

Beyond presence and beyond this reality is imagination. I love what Albus Dumbledore said to Harry Potter when Harry asked him if what he was experiencing at that moment was just inside his head. He answered him, "Of course this is happening inside your head Harry, but why on earth should that mean it is not real?" Reality is perception. And perception is different for every person. And by virtue of this fact, religion can never be based in reality.

Chapter 13

Distinguishing the Voice of God Within

"Your vision will become clearer only when you look into your heart. Who looks outside, dreams; who looks inside, awakens."

-Karl Jung

Be Still and Hear Him

Oh that I might understand,

God within and so expand,

Across the nations to every land

Be still! Be still! And hear him!

God, He speaks inside your soul;

His word is present and takes control;

Go within and you'll be whole;

Be still! Be still! And hear him!

Too many times we search without,

And hear the preacher who loves to shout;

But this is not what God's about;

Be still! Be still! And hear him!

Heaven's not so far away,

When you invite the Lord to stay;

From within he'll hear you pray;

Be still! Be still! And hear him!

Go within and shut the door;

Meet him there, he'll not ignore;

Your hope, your joy he will restore;

Be still! Be still! And hear him!

Oh the sweetness of his voice,

And to know that you're his choice;

He will make your heart rejoice;

Be still! Be still! And hear him!

In the midst of all the clamoring voices competing for my allegiance, I hungered for just one solitary voice- the voice of God within. A prayer swelled inside my heart and parted these lips in a desperate plea, *"Oh God, please help me to discern your voice above all the others. I want to hear from you and you alone."* Not just once, not twice, not three times, did this cry for discernment erupt, but day after day, as the competing voices became more confusing.

I had no idea what this voice was supposed to feel like or sound like; But I was sure that it was in there, among all the noise and confusion. I knew that God had said, *"Be still and know that I am God."* (Psalms 46:10) I understood that after the conversion of the apostle Paul he, *"conferred not* (Did not consult with) *with flesh and blood,"* (with people) but was alone for several years, listening to God's voice within. (Acts 1 & 2) I knew that Moses heard the voice of God alone in the desert; Elijah heard the voice of God after the tempest had past and all was still; Jesus got away alone to commune with God. So two things were certain; 1) I needed to get away from as many competing voices as possible, and 2) I needed to quiet my mind- to be still and listen for his voice. Neither of these two factors would prove to be an easy undertaking.

A healing crisis from childhood trauma and abuse is about one of the most soul wracking, heart wrenching journeys one could embark upon. It takes so much courage and tenacity to see it through to complete deliverance from all the fears, lies, and control over your life. Having entered this journey myself, hearing the voice of God became paramount in my life.

At first, I thought it was just me, just thoughts inside my own head. But this *one voice* began to stand out among them all. It felt like my own thoughts, but conversed with me as if it were a second person. It was not audible, *but it was real.* I began to pay attention to this ongoing conversation within. The more I tuned into this little voice within, the more I realized it was like Jiminy Cricket- like a little friend, talking to me, guiding me, like a lamp in the darkness. (Psalms 119:105) Then, opportunities would arise to put it to the test and follow its leading. Each time I followed its very clear instructions, it always proved to be the right way, and slowly I began to gain confidence in it.

This little voice spoke with so much love. Guidance was given in such a tender way. It became a joy to know it and to follow it, because its ways were the ways of peace. It led me through the darkest valleys, and over the most difficult mountains- safe and secure! It comforted me when no one else was there. It poured oil and wine into my wounded heart. The doubts I had about it in the beginning melted away each time I listened and it proved its source to be that of Spirit.

It felt so much like my own thoughts, that, in the beginning I really believed it was. But then one day it conveyed the message to me, that God speaks to us in our own personal language- a language that we completely understand. It's not just (in my case) English. But it is the way *I personally use English* and how I personally understand it. God knows our language. (Acts 2:6)

So intimate was this little voice; Sometimes it would speak things that I would think*, surely that cannot be God*. An example is, one day I was outside my city of residence. I was in the middle of a very intense healing crisis, and had been crying all morning. I had to go out and run some errands. I was driving around with a foggy and muddled mind, when the voice within began to tell me exactly which direction to go, where to turn, and which stores to go to. I just followed it, because at the time, I could not think clearly. Step by step, it led me through my errands and brought me home quickly. I was truly amazed. I just listened and followed. On days when I felt overwhelmed and did not know where to begin, I would go in and kneel and pray and ask for its guidance. Then I would be still and listen and sure enough, that still small voice would begin to speak. *"Go in and load your dishwasher and wipe down your counters Liz, and then meet me back here again."* I would carefully follow its instructions, and then go back, and it would tell me what to do next. And my day would run smoothly and I my heart would return to still waters. Not always have I needed this detailed leading, but when I have, *it's never, ever failed me.*

It is also a voice of conscience. It would check me about things I was about to say, and I would shut my mouth. It would soothe me when I felt self-hatred; it would talk to me of its love for me, *how precious I was.* Oh how I needed to hear that. I felt so loved by this inner guide, so watched over, so cared for; It knew me so intimately, and lead me through life so lovingly, like a nurse that cherishes her children, (1 Thessalonians 2:7) that before long, I knew, beyond the shadow of a doubt, this was none other than *the voice of God within.*

Since I have come to know and trust my inner guide, I have discovered a soul-freedom I never dreamed possible. I have come to know true love and acceptance, first for myself and then for others as well. My heart is lighter and my vision clearer than ever before. I have entered into God's rest- the blessed assurance that nothing can separate me from the love of God!

Find the Voice of God within you. You will not regret it. Begin by asking him to help you discern his voice above all others. Be open to his leading and guiding hand. Doubts will come. It will not come easy, but come it will. God is faithful. This is why Christ came and died and rose again- to bless us with this special, divine, and Holy Communion with the voice of God within. There is no other friend as precious as God himself, dwelling within.

The voice of God within is a very compassionate voice. The Holy Spirit is a giving spirit, and is contrasted with a thief that comes to steal, to kill and to destroy. The Holy Spirit comes, which is Christ, which is God- all one in the same thing, to give us life and to give it more abundantly. So when we are listening within and learning to distinguish the voice of God within, that voice will always be a comforting voice. Yes, it can be a voice of warning as well. It may warn us to be careful about someone, or it may check us when we are about to do something. It can say within us, "no, don't do that." But it is never a condemning, angry voice. And it's not a voice that will tell us to do any of the things that the thief does. It's not going to tell you to steal, it's not going to tell you to kill and it's not going to tell you to destroy anything about you or somebody else. If a voice is leading you in these ways, most definitely it will be causing you distress, and if a voice or thought pattern is causing you distress, it's not the voice of God within you.

When you are aligned with the true voice of God within you, that brings complete *peace;* that alignment is what gives us strength, and peace and purpose and it balances us. So if there is a voice inside of us that is just wreaking havoc, then it is just a voice that is a part of the constant chatter that is going on in our head. It may be a voice of influence from something recorded years ago. We've recorded in our minds many messages; we have songs that go through our head and such. So when you want to know whether or not something is the voice of God and you're trying to hear God's voice within, more than anything it is going to feel like a familiar friend. It's going to feel like somebody that comes into your life and you can just be yourself with; you know you don't have to hide *anything* from this friend, because this friend is so familiar with you and they love you and accept you just as you are. They are not there to judge you and to make you feel bad. That is not what God's voice is there for. I have never found the real voice of God inside my heart to be condemning and judgmental. But I have found that type of condemning and judgmental voice outside- people that claim to be the voice for God or to be speaking on behalf of God, bring a lot of judgement and a lot of condemnation. But when I am in tune to God's voice with in my own heart, it never feels that way to me. It feels very gentle, very loving, and very strong and powerful It makes me feel strong, protected and cared about.

The voice of God within will challenge you sometimes because it wants to see you grow. Life is all about growth. We know that anything that stops growing becomes stagnant and starts to die. So this voice may challenge you. But it's not going to put distress on you. That was another problem I had to deal with at church. The voices without, that were claiming to be speaking on behalf of God, were distressing me. They were asking of me things that distressed me and that didn't resonate with me such as, to go knock on doors and try to tell people about the church and about salvation. And when you want to live for God, and you want to please him, you do those things that are asked of you when you believe that it comes from God; but it was distressful.

It doesn't mean that God's voice will never lead us into a place that there might be a struggle. But there is a real difference between a struggle and feeling distressed. God's voice is there to give us more abundant life; it's there to bring us peace; it's there to bring us joy. These are the fruits of Spirit- goodness, and joy, and peace and love . . . and Christ taught that is how we know that we are connected within is when we have these fruits coming out. But when you have the opposite of these coming out, you are misaligned with God's spirit somewhere. We all become misaligned at times- that's just part of the struggle of life. It doesn't mean that God's spirit left us, it just means we are misaligned with it; we are following other chatter rather than that voice within that is trying to guide us and direct us and help us to grow and help us to be happy and help us to be centered and help us to get the most out of this life experience here on earth.

Exercise:

Begin paying attention to the dialogue in your head. Ask Spirit to give you discernment of to know its voice. There will be a resonance within, something that will tell you; this is the voice to follow- this is right leading.

As you develop trust in this inner voice, you will develop self-trust. You will begin to reclaim your life.

Chapter 14

What Listening Within Has Taught Me

"A thousand times we die in one life. We crumble, break and tear apart until the layers of illusion are burned away, and all that is left, is the truth of who and what we really are."

-Teal Swan

Leaving the religion I had endorsed for so many years and slowly letting go of beliefs that no longer served me, left me in a sort of limbo state. I thought, okay, so now I understand what I *don't* believe, but now I need to figure out what I *do* believe. I had been so long identified with being a member of this particular church and I really no longer identified with its teachings at my core. I knew people were watching me slowly change and wondering where I now stood. But in all honesty, I did not even know where I stood. I sort of kept up this weak façade of the faith I once claimed for the sake of not being questioned or challenged or harassed. I cut online social ties with most of the people that still identified with what I came out of in order to help decrease the anxiety over this limbo state that I now felt I was in.

People generally want to pin you down on what you believe. Who are you? What are you? What is your belief? Are you an agnostic or an atheist? Do you believe in Christ?

Well yeah…

But to you believe that he is the only begotten Son of God, that he is the only way to heaven?

So you're a Christian. Are you a modern Christian or fundamental Christian?

It's like they just want to be able to label you and stick you in a box, and say, this is what you are. We all do this to one degree of another because it helps us to be able to make sense of life; patterns are normal in nature. When we break things down even to the atom, we see certain patterns all throughout creation. People are drawn to patterns and they want to be able to see that you fit a certain pattern. And even for ourselves, we often feel a sense of identity when we fit into certain frameworks of patterns.

But I am learning that identity has nothing to do with reality. Identity is just something of this earth-plane existence. It is what a lot of spiritualist call "ego." For example, some of my ego identities are, I am a mom; I have three children; I'm a wife; I'm a student of psychology; an ego identity is the vehicle in which we learn important lessons through. Some spiritual teachers believe that we need to get rid of the ego or get the ego out of the way. But I do not personally believe that. I believe that the ego is for us to inhabit and learn through. The ego is what embodies this experience we have here. But perhaps some came here to live amongst egotistical humanity and learn to be completely separated from their personal ego. I have not gotten to that place in my spiritual walk. I don't see that yet. I see the ego as something that personifies our experience here.

Not too long ago I had this night vision- like a dream, but yet it was not a dream; it was more of a vision- or an out of body experience. I was standing outside my body and I was looking at my body as it was floating inside of this large vortex. It was floating around in space, empty- like a dead body or a sleeping body. It kind of reminded me of that scene from the movie Maleficent when she puts Aurora into a sleep and floats her over to the enchanted forest. So, I was standing outside the vortex and atop of it and there were two spiritual beings on either side of me, and we were having a very intellectual conversation. It was like my knowing was way

128

beyond what I have here because of the veil. And we were discussing the experience I was having inside of this ego I have here- Elizabeth. I do not remember the content of the conversation nor do I recall what the beings looked like. I know that they were very spiritual and highly evolved. And I still felt like I had this same consciousness, but at the same time, I was separate from Elizabeth. And Elizabeth was the subject of our discussion- this person that I inhabit here. We were reviewing where I was, what I had experienced being Elizabeth and what I was learning from this experience. I knew too, that I was going to have to go back into that body- that I was not finished here. And I remember feeling a little distressed about that because this was a hard experience for me, and I had to just be resolved to finish this life time out.

I have struggled immensely since I have come into this world; it's just been a very difficult place for me to be in since I was really little and many, many times I have just looked around and thought, what am I doing here? And I have so often felt mortified about how people treat each other here. This experience here on earth has been tough. There have been really beautiful and special times in my life too and I think this experience has been very educational. I have learned a lot and grown so much in this life experience. But my point is that after that vision- *I knew...* I knew when I woke up that I was having an earth experience here and that *I was an evolving being-* I wasn't just created a new here. However, Elizabeth was. She was just created. But my soul came into this experience, into this physical body.

From personal study and research and soul searching- from studying different philosophies, theologies, and religions across the world rather than just being stuck in the one that my culture is embedded in- and most importantly from listening to and trusting the voice of God within, I have come to believe very differently than when I was going to church. At this point in my life experience, I could really never go back to a Christian church and just enter in there and be a part of that. I feel like I have evolved past that phase of my existence. But please don't shut me out now. Hear me out.

Spirit has shown me that I was not even expected to evolve past that phase within this life time. Here is what I have come to understand thus far from what Spirit has taught me. We all know of a certainty that one day this body will cease to function and we will die to this ego experience. Have you ever wondered why we don't just keep living and just keep growing and evolving in this life? Why do we have to go through the death process? I have come to believe that my soul is ever growing, learning and evolving. One reason we die is so we can begin a new life experience and learn through different perspectives. So why can't we just move across the world and go into a different culture? To a certain extent we can. But when you have a huge paradigm shift beyond the culture that you have been conditioned in, it is almost impossible for you to continue to live. You are so misplaced from what you came here to experience. You came here to experience a certain aspect of this life. For example, I was born here in a Christian based culture and in a bible believing family. I have experienced fully what it is to be a Christian and to believe in Jesus Christ as my personal Savior, etc.… *I was born into this culture*. This culture shaped my experience and my beliefs about myself, God, life and the world I live in. If I were to go live across the world as a Muslim, in a Muslim culture, I would probably not do too well, because of my conditioning and predisposition towards that culture. And even if I did, I would still be filtering everything I saw and experienced through the filters of the ego I have come to identify with.

Death is a reset button. Death is necessary in order to *reset* my program. I die, I review this life experience and what I learned from it, and now I can reset and evolve from there. It's sort of like a computer program that is full of data and cannot really take anymore, sometimes you have to remove the old and reset the entire program. That is what death is for. I believe we have a life plan and goals when we come here.

But when I experienced a major paradigm shift during this lifetime, it was as if my reset button kicked in *before* I died, and it was unexpected. It's now difficult for me to find a place where I am at currently to continue to grow like I would if I had been reset and then placed in a completely different environment. I hope you can follow what I am saying. Again, this is where I am and what I believe and it may not resonate with you. That is okay. I have found when spirit teaches you, it is very often difficult to transfer the message in an understandable fashion to others. Language is actually a huge barrier. Spirit more often than not speaks in knowing. It is an understanding- a download that we now have to transfer into our language in order to share.

I do not feel like I am better than others; I believe people can be wiser or more knowledgeable in certain areas, but there is always somebody else that is wiser or more knowledgeable in other areas. I do not believe those things make a soul more valuable than another soul. Like I said before, we are *all* teachers and we are *all* students *all* of the time. I don't care who you are- even if you have been a negative or a horrible person, you are still a valuable soul- and still evolving.

I have more beliefs and theories about all of this and more that I am learning. But this belief system that I now have and inhabit, because I have not been through the reset death process, it has been really difficult for me to fully embody it. I feel almost like I am living in two different worlds. I have that Elizabeth ego still that was so set on the Christian culture, but yet this other self...

It's not that I don't believe in the Christian culture anymore. I believe that it is very important. The Christian culture is an important stepping stone for people's evolution. It definitely has been very valuable in my evolution. I do believe that there was a man called Jesus and that he was anointed the Christ and that he did die on a cross- and as I have explained it here in this book, is how I believe it. I believe that there was a very important purpose for him being here. I believe that at any given time I can call his name and he will be here for me. I believe he is a very highly evolved and perfected soul. The Bible says he was made perfect through the things which he suffered. And that is what I believe we are all evolving towards is that perfection. Maybe some Christians get to that perfection within their Christian experience. Maybe that wasn't enough to get me there- I don't know at this point.

I don't claim to understand everything. But this belief that I now inhabit makes sense to me- it *resonates* within me. When I just believed the teaching of Christianity, a *lot* of it didn't make sense to me. I love a lot about it; that is why I held onto it. I love the part of loving and being good and having a clean life and treating people right. Those are all aspects that I loved about it. And I love the thought of Jesus and what he did for humanity and how much love and sacrifice he put into his life here— how he suffered because of his love for us. That is all so beautiful and precious.

Yet there was so much about the Christian teachings that just didn't make any sense to me. So much that I just was buying into by "faith" – *blind* faith. That is why I gave some of the exercises in this book so you can do a little soul searching yourself. What is it that you love about your beliefs and what is it that you are just taking on that you don't even know why? I personally got to the place that I had to get to the core of okay, what do *I* believe? There was so much about what was being drilled into me for years that just didn't make any sense. One example was the teaching of heaven and hell. It was easy to think that somebody like Hitler who was responsible for so many atrocities, being in a place of everlasting torture. But, the religion I was in and many other Christian religions, if you were not a part of that particular religion, you would go to hell. Numerous times the pastor stated that there are many sincere souls in hell. And that just bothered my mind that a good and loving God would just send people to this place of eternal torment because they missed the mark. It just seemed so cruel to me, and it didn't make sense. And the unfairness of it all- someone is born in war-torn society and watches their parents be blown to pieces and picks around garbage to survive- contrast that experience to an American born free man who has loving "Christian" parents. The first grows embittered and the later grows and has a happy life and "serves God"- where is the fairness that the one born into hell, is now thrown into an eternal hell? I'm sorry something is missing when my love and compassion begins to surpass what the God I am being taught to honor is.

So are many things that didn't make sense about the Christian teaching. People tried to make sense of it- "well God knows the heart, that person was given a chance, God is faithful to every soul etc...." I do believe that the God, the energy of God is faithful. I don't doubt that part. But there was just so much that didn't make sense. But what I have now, the beliefs I have now- they resonate with me, where before they didn't.

Now, the age-old teaching of reincarnation, which was part of the early Christian teachings, makes *complete* sense to me. And I didn't just say, "Oh I think reincarnation makes sense I think I will believe that." That would just be blind faith again. I was afraid to believe in anything. But what I did was some researching. I read a book about reincarnation written by a doctor who didn't even believe in the afterlife but wrote about his experiences that brought him to believe in it later. It was his experiences with patients who had died and been brought back to life and the commonality of it and why he went beyond thinking that this is just a brain thing; this is something that is *real.* There was so much about their stories that defied the things I was taught in Christianity. Heaven wasn't just barred off for a certain group of people. He studied hundreds of death experiences and they were experiencing the same patterns- a life review, a light, a beautiful place, being told they were not finished here, and such. I watched videos of true accounts of really young children starting from infanthood who talked about being in other lives. I was obsessed with the program "Ghost inside My Child" that had parents of these children recount their amazing stories. It fascinated me. I also have read several books about people who have seen ghosts or spirits since they were children. I read about what they learned about the afterlife through this conduit. I believe these were born into this world for that very purpose, to help people reconnect and to teach people that there is a life after death and to help humanity here to evolve.

Do I know everything? No, absolutely not! Do I expect you to believe what I believe? No! That is not the point of this book. Rather, I wrote this book to synthesize and process my spiritual experience and to share that with others and to challenge them to dare to trust the voice of God inside even when it goes outside the box of their current understanding. If you are a Christian, this book may have just agitated you enough to want to delve further into your beliefs and get a more solid hold on it. You may not feel like doing anything different. Or for some, this may have been a ho-hum read. Everyone is different and no two perspectives are alike.

I have not purposed to change somebodies belief system or to shame Christianity. I feel there are many aspects about Christianity that are good and that help people and have even rescued many out of horrible destructive life patterns. So I believe it does a lot of good. But it's a *belief system* and once any belief system puts a cap on and says, "This is it, you cannot grow beyond what we believe," souls are hindered- tremendously!

When I first left the Christian religion I was with, I was so *conditioned* to believe certain ways, and one of the teachings that bound me up in so much fear was that, "you have left God's church and therefore you have left God." And I was struggling so much to overcome fear.

A few months after I left, I had to have a hysterectomy and a couple in Africa, bless their souls, were fasting and praying for me. During this six hour surgery I was blessed with a heavenly visit. I was surrounded with these heavenly beings that were like little children yet they were very intelligent and mature. They had the spirit and purity of little innocent children. They were joyful and playful and excited to be with me, and I felt so immensely happy and peaceful and *loved so completely.* It was like my whole entire spirit that had been struggling and was just starving for some kind of affirmation and love out there, was now being flooded with this adoring heavenly visit. They just came in and literally saturated my soul with love while I was in surgery.

I do not remember all that we chatted about, but I do remember one part of in which they very clearly told me something concerning a teaching at the church I had come out of. This teaching was that if you sin, or you are a sinner, your prayers are not heard. God does not listen to a sinner. They emphatically stated many times, "If you are sinning your prayers are not going any higher than the ceiling. You need to repent of your sins in order for God to hear your prayers." And they backed it up with things they read from the Bible. However, in this visitation I was experiencing, these little beings were so concerned about that teaching. And they were telling me that it was so *"toxic."* That is the word they used- that it was so toxic to people. I never forgot this- the way they were explaining this to me was so saturated with love. It wasn't like they were angry at people or at the church for teaching this. It was more that they were so *genuinely concerned* that I understood the harm of this teaching and that it was not true, and that I conveyed the message to others that God *does* hear prayers, and that prayers are so important. And not to just stop praying because you think you're a sinner or because you think you are doing wrong. They were so concerned because to believe this is severing such an important connection for humanity- to tell somebody that their prayers cannot reach God. They were so concerned that I let people know that prayer is a life-line and they can pray *anytime.* That is what Christ came to do was to connect people and to say, God is there for you. And not to teach them that they can't get to God. This was just such an important message from them.

And another thing that they made known to me was that I was doing well. They reassured me like nothing else- "You're doing so good Liz. You are right where you need to be." It was like they *bolstered* me. And this too was really important. It has been said when you get a heavenly visit like that, it is usually because you are going to go through something really difficult, and you need strength and they are bringing strength to you. Sure enough it was not long after this visit, I had a very difficult situation come up that challenged me and if I had not had this encouraging heavenly visit, I could have gone spiraling into a deep abyss of despair of thinking that God doesn't love me at all; that I had done so wrong leaving church. But because of what I experienced, I was able to hold onto God's love and to know when this came against me that it was not true.

I have come to realize, especially through my relationships with others, that there is no way that somebody else can see through *my* eyes, or feel through my emotions- nor I theirs. We can get a sense of what another person is feeling and what they are seeing, through observation and tuning into them- we can *empathize* with them; but that is still our own ego perspective of them.   .

In Spirit, everything is one- Spirit animates every ego in this universe. So Spirit knows what the ego perspectives are, because Spirit is in every ego. I don't believe that God is just a presence that sits in heaven on a literal throne just for judgement sake and enjoying all the worship of the beings he created, and waiting for the rest of us to decide to choose him or not. I believe God is spirit; I believe it's the energy that animates everything in this world, which brought it into being.

Before I understood this, one time I was on a walk and I was during the middle of my healing crisis. I was praying and talking to God. I was saying to him, "How can you, who sits in a beautiful paradise called heaven, and is all powerful, who can do whatever you want, how can you possibly understand what it's really like for me here? What I am going through, how can you fully understand that?" I was praying this way because I was looking at God through very egotistical eyes. I didn't really understand Spirit at all. But Spirit was about to give me a small glimpse into what it truly is. As I listened to the voice of God within, it spoke to my heart and answered my question. Spirit impressed upon me that day that spirit is in everyone- it's in every perspective. Spirit *is* every perspective. So spirit feels *everything* that *every* ego feels-ever! Every person that has sat in a concentration camp, every person that has ever been crucified, every one that has been sexually abused, every person who has been beaten or lynched, every person who has had acid thrown in their face because of their beliefs, every person who has been sold into brothels, every person on the famine fields, every child who has been abducted, every person who has been buried alive, etc.... every perspective- Spirit didn't just go in there as an observer; Spirit is in it and *feels* it all.

So in that respect, we are gods. That is why Jesus said, "Don't you know it is written in your words, you are gods?" We are gods because we are all a part of that same spirit that is God. We are all one in that spirit. But our *egos* are separate. They are separate perspectives. In heaven and in spirit, there is perfect unity-perfect oneness. But here there are egos.

A lot of this I have learned through the darkest days of my healing process. When you are healing from abuse, you are tapping into and facing very real and haunting memories and thoughts that were formed and have taken deep root inside your heart, that you are *worthless* and that you are *unloveable.* And let me tell you, it is *so painful* when you go back to heal. You just want to cling to anybody that will love you and yet your trust is so wary.

I had clung to this one person whom I had learned to have a certain amount of trust in. This person offered me understanding and the attention that I hungered for. For nearly four years, this person patiently listened and consoled me and tried to help me through. But when a change in life events came and it was time for this person to move on, emotionally I snapped- I just could not handle it yet. Nonetheless, there was something deep inside of me that knew that Spirit was working because I had been praying that God would break that neediness within- that tendency to be so clingy. I knew that it was unhealthy and I knew that this person could not just carry me the rest of their life and I felt like I was just sucking the life out of this person holding on so tight. But I was dealing with some extremely deep-seeded abandonment issues and it was so emotionally wracking for me. I was grappling not only with the fact that this person was no longer going to be there for me in the way that I felt like I needed, I was beginning to realize that this person really did *not* understand, even after being in there with me for those past few years, the depth of what I was wrestling with. Suddenly there was this deep gulf between us that I had not felt before.

One day, while I was in the midst of this deep grief of separation, God began to speak to my heart as I was driving. I often talk with God when I am in my car alone. On this particular day I was praying and God just started talking to me. And Spirit said to me, "Liz, I know what you are going through right now is very, very, hard. And I am here with you. I haven't left you. I will never leave you nor forsake you." God is just so sweet and compassionate; knowing how sensitive I was of abandonment and feeling so fresh the sting of this newest separation, often he reminded me that he would never leave me nor forsake me.

"I know that you are having a difficult time, but you are going to come through it. I want you to know something. In heaven- when you get to the other side- it's going to be so different. There is closeness, a unity, a bond, in heaven that surpasses anything that anyone has ever experienced here on earth; Mother and child, husband and wife, soul mates- it surpasses it all. Even if you could obtain the closest unbreakable bond with someone here, it will eventually end. But in heaven, the bond surpasses it all of that and there are no break-ups."

I could not even fully grasp what God was trying to express to me. It was such a foreign thought; but yet, I knew that Spirit was conveying this insight into my experience to help comfort me through this dissolution. I felt an emotional umbilical cord had been severed. And God was giving me something to hold onto so I that I would not give in completely to despair, because I got dangerously depressed at times. Spirit was trying to help me by impressing me with the hope to come of oneness- that absence of separation or abandonment.

Two year later now, I have completely healed of that divide that happened there. And I feel closer to God- not in a religious, pious sense; but rather it's a *knowing* deep inside of my soul, that

God is with me and that he will never leave me and that he loves me. And that no matter what comes against me, I know now that it is coming from outside of me, but what is inside of me, *what is within- nothing can touch*. Nobody can put their finger on that. Like the Bible says, nothing can separate me from the love of God; No thought, no doubt, no religious belief, no action- nothing can separate me from the love that God has. That love is so pure and so *unconditional*. God's love is *not* conditional.

That was another teaching I had to unlearn. In the church that I went to I was taught that God's love is conditional. But God has shown me beyond any shadow of doubt, that the spirit of God is *pure* love. And pure love is *never* conditional. It just loves. And it understands perfectly because the spirit is in every perspective. Spirit understands the intricacies of why that ego perspective is where it is and does what it does. There is no psychologist, scientist, or theologies- no group of people that could ever pick apart another ego and understand it fully. But Spirit does because Spirit is 100% *within* every ego perspective.

Morning Sunlight

Waking to Sunlight stretched across my bed
God's creation merrily dances
to the songs that the winged creatures bring
in the dawn of hope and more chances

All of my senses are born on a prayer
the tiniest speck twinkles with delight
Time to arise and face a new day
God lifts me into the sunlight

"You're doing well, you've grown more than expected"
Spirit whispers strength into my soul
the voice within speaks the wisdom of sages
and mirrors the way to live life to the full

"Children run before thinking and stumble along
Careless of life till they fall
Masters think before acting, and all that they do
is authentic and considerate of all"

Awake to the calls in the greeting of day
the sunlight of Spirit shows no form
yet a peaceful calm sweeps over my being
Sustained in the eye of the storm

No word of man, no scornful eye
No judgement or wrathful requite
Nothing can separate me from God
or the gift of the morning sunlight

Epilogue

If you are reading this book, it is no accident or chance. I do not believe that anybody that is solid within their own belief system, wherever they are at right now, picked up this book, thumbed through it, read what it was about, and decided to read it if they were 100% satisfied with their experience with God. Unless it's just someone who has an agenda to find fault or pick apart what is in it, just for the sake of argument.

Like I said before, my point here isn't to defame Christianity or any other religion. I no longer call myself a "Christian" in the modern sense of the term. But as this book has clearly pointed out, I believe in Christ and I often pray in his name. I totally believe that we have a record of Jesus for a reason. I do not think that this record of the Bible, these collected letters written to different people are for not. I believe they have a lot to teach us. I have studied the Bible thoroughly for years; I don't just cast that all off and say, "Oh I don't believe that anymore." I believe in the cause of Christ Jesus.

But I do not call myself a "Christian," because it's a label and it comes with a lot of connotations that I do not want to be attached to. And so I have separated myself from that. And the reality is I do not want to be attached to any spiritual labels that are out there at this point in my experience here on earth. I don't want to be called a new-ager, or a Buddhist, or you're one of those Christian Science people, etc....

I have pooled different perspectives from within all those religions. I have discovered so many good and enlightening perspectives and interesting facts. And I have found really good and resonating teachings and enlightenment in places that have no overt claims on spirituality. Everything in this world has the potential to teach and enlighten us- autobiographies, mythologies, fairytales, fictions- but I have whittled down the whole idea of belief and faith enough to say, as my friend so wisely answered me all those years ago, *"Life is a mystery, and I am okay with that."*

I'm okay! I no longer am full of fearful woe that I may not figure this life thing out right, and I might find out in the end that I was deceived, and God may cast me out of heaven forever and put me in a fiery burning furnace of endless torture. *"Oh no, what if I am wrong and I was supposed to just believe in Jesus alone and now I am not right with God... blah...blah...blah!"* I don't fear those things anymore. Those are no longer a part of my experience here. They come knocking on my door, but I just ignore them. I just say, you know what, that is not a part of me anymore. I don't buy into that anymore. I don't believe that I have to be coerced by fear into a belief system. And now when I feel that something is trying to put fear in me, whether a belief system or anything else, - *this is where fear has become a really **beautiful tool** of mine.*

When you feel fear trying to pull you into something, you can know right then that is *manipulation*. And that it is something you need to back away from and *not* do or buy into, because it is not something genuine and authentic from your soul; it is fear. And so you back off of it realizing that fear is just trying to work on you. This could be peer fear and so many other types of fears- it is a powerhouse of a tool. I have learned to use this powerful emotional tool, to my advantage. Fear manipulated and ruled my life for so long and now I have taken this ruler off of its throne and subjected it to *my* rule. I am ruling my fear. *I am using my fear with amazing results.*

Learning to use fear as a tool was another part of my spiritual evolution. We are co-creators in our life, made in God's image and he is a creator. We co-create our lives by our thoughts and our words. I am evolving, I am learning and I wanted to share my experience in hope that my experience might ignite or flame the internal fires of others; that something will be here that they can draw from.

We are all in different places and our journey is our own. We all have filters and we either approach new thoughts with curiosity and a willingness to learn and expand, or we place judgement on things that do not fit through our filters. Fear rules and we decide to allow the voice of judgement to guide us- in order that new information does not mess up our filters (E.g. they just have a bad spirit; they are really out there; they are an anti-Christ; they are possessed, etc...). Judgement is placed on what we don't understand and are afraid of. A label is attached and it is all written off. It's a personal choice.

For many years I wrote many things off that came my way; because I had fears that were keeping me locked within the religious filters I had been conditioned by. Fear is a *powerful* master. Fear keeps us earth-bound, and caged. And it's through breaking that chain of fear that our spirit can soar. The cage is open, but there is an invisible chain of fear that keeps us bound to the cage. God hands us the tool to break the chain, and the tool is *courage*. God says, "break that chain with your courage." And it's at that point we can take the tool and do the work or we can back away and say, no, I can't do that right now. It is our choice. We can stay within our filters where we feel safe our entire life. Or we can say, you know, I am ready; I am ready to use my courage, I am ready to master fear and I'm ready to evolve further and to learn more. I am ready to trust the voice of God within my own soul. That is a decision each one of us has to make for our self.

Namaste! I acknowledge Spirit in you and Spirit in me!

About the Author

Elizabeth Van Cleve is an intuitive-empathic and is currently studying psychology in California. She lives with her husband and special needs daughter.

www.hivbeslife.com

51294945R00085